*Dynamic Women®*

# TRAILBLAZER Secrets!

Top Thought Leaders, Experts &
Dynamic Women®
Share their Stories &
Secrets on Being a Trailblazer!

Featuring
## Diane Rolston
and 42 other Leading
Entrepreneurs & Professionals

Copyright © 2024 Diane Rolston
All rights reserved.

# DEDICATION

This book is dedicated to all the Dynamic Women® out there and those who raised them:

*

The ones who go for it, even when others say they can't.

*

The ones who give a hand up when they are asked.

*

The ones who ask for help, guidance & whatever they need.

*

The ones who are fearless on the outside, yet fearful inside.

*

The ones who choose to change & those forced to change.

*

The ones who are awarded & those who silently excel.

*

The ones who lead the way & those who support them.

*

The ones who blaze a trail, speak up & don't take crap.

*

The ones who listen openly, cry hard, & love unconditionally.

*

The ones who know they're Dynamic & those who don't realize it yet.

*

The ones who are You!

# WHAT OTHERS ARE SAYING ABOUT DIANE ROLSTON and THIS BOOK

*"This is a wonderful book that shows you immediately how to be happier and fulfill your unlimited potential."*

~ **Brian Tracy,** Speaker, Author, Consultant

*"Diane is an amazing woman that does incredible work helping women develop, especially entrepreneurs, high-level, high-performing women, develop holistic lives of balance. Not just balanced, but really balancing all the different aspects of your life, not just one thing, but so many parts of yourself, and working with assistance, and really helping you realize you can afford it, you cannot not afford it. I want to encourage you to reach out not only for her work, but also for the community that she's created for people who are part of that work going forward so you have a supportive community to take you to the next level. So anyway, take advantage for work, check out her website, check out her get in touch with her and I promise you, you'll be glad you did."*

~ **Jack Canfield,** Author and Motivational Speaker
Co-Creator of the "Chicken Soup for the Soul" book series
Featured teacher in the movie "The Secret"

*"Our long-term goals for our audience were met and we received very positive feedback about the event including, "Empowering, Inspirational & Fun!" If the women in your community are ready to be recharged and inspired, I would recommend Diane Rolston for your next event."*

~ **Mae Legg,** Senior Small Business Consultant
Brantford-Brant Business Resource Centre

*"Diane provides you with a roadmap for achieving your goals!"*
~ **Joe Theismann**, Legendary NFL World Champion Quarterback & Entrepreneur

*"If you want to have major breakthroughs and overcome adversity and take your life to new levels of success, love, joy, happiness, and fulfillment, and you want to have great success as an entrepreneur as a businessperson, then you've got to work with my good friend Diane Rolston. Diane is not only she's smart, and not only does she have strategies and life experiences that will inspire you and help you. But Diane truly comes from the heart. Diane is a giver. She's a server, and she's on a mission to change lives and she will make your life better. And if you want to learn how to become more productive, if you want to learn how to become more effective. And if you want to learn how to you know, outsource those tasks and those things that are just weighing you down and causing you to not get things done that cause you to waste time, energy money and to add more stress to your life. Then you've got to work with Diane and allow her to help outsource to folks who can get those things done for you. If you're ready to have major breakthroughs and if you're ready to become more productive, more efficient, and more effective, then work with my good friend Diane Rolston today. You will be so thankful and grateful you did."*
~ **James Malinchak**, Featured on ABCs Hit TV Show "Secret Millionaire", Keynote Speakers & Business Coach

*"I have participated in Diane's Dynamic Women® groups over the last few years for continued personal and professional development. Diane's high energy and co-active coaching skills are utilized in this group setting as they are in her Dynamic Year program. I would highly recommend working with Diane on goal setting as she has the experience, an encouraging way, and cuts through to the crux of the matter."*
~ **Kirsten Anderson**, Founder Integrate Play Solutions

"Diane Rolston is of the most engaging and positive speakers on leadership and success."
~ **Kevin Harrington,** Original Shark from Shark Tank, Inventor of the Infomercial

"Diane has been my coach and I have grown so much through my work with her. When I started, I was looking to launch my business and with her help, I launched. I really couldn't have got there without her help. Diane is a fabulous coach who lovingly challenges you to move towards your dream life. She is honest and direct with your best interests in mind. Her various programs (Dynamic You, Dynamic Year, Dynamic Balance, Dynamic Business Success Formula, and others) have all been extremely helpful in my growth both in business and in my personal life. Thanks, Diane, for all your help."
~ **Brenda Benham**, Presentation Specialist

"I have been working with Diane for a few years now both in Dynamic Women (her sharing sessions are legendary) and as a client. Her masterminds are simply amazing! This year I became an Elite Coaching Client and the result still amazes me - I've worked through skills, concepts, and so much more to develop my business model. She is incredibly patient, knowledgeable, helpful, professional, kind, genuine and really cares about the success of each of her clients. I cannot recommend Diane enough. I thank Diane for all that she has given me - support, an ear, expertise, plus much more as I navigate this new world of business. I highly recommend her."
~ **Kathy Fester**, Chief Gratitude Officer of K.I.T. (Keep in Touch) Communication

"**Learning**
IS **FUEL** FOR
**MOTIVATION.**"
~ Diane Rolston

Copyright © 2024 Diane Rolston

ALL RIGHTS RESERVED. No part of this book or its associated ancillary materials may be reproduced or transmitted to any form or by any means, electronic or mechanical, including photocopying, recording, or by any informational storage or retrieval system without permission from the publisher.

PUBLISHED BY: Diane Rolston

DISCLAIMER AND/OR LEGAL NOTICES

While all attempts have been made to verify information provided in this book and its ancillary materials, neither the author or publisher assumes any responsibility for errors, inaccuracies or omissions and is not responsible for any financial loss by customer in any manner. Any slights of people or organizations are unintentional. If advice concerning legal, financial, accounting or related matters is needed, the services of a qualified professional should be sought This book and its associated ancillary materials, including verbal and written training, is not intended for use as a source of legal, financial or accounting advice. You should be aware of the various laws governing business transactions or other business practices in your particular geographical location.

EARNINGS & INCOME DISCLAIMER

With respect to the reliability, accuracy, timeliness, usefulness, adequacy, completeness, and/or suitability of information provided in this book, Diane Rolston, its partners, associates, affiliates, consultants, and/or presenters, make no warranties, guarantees, representations or claims of any kind. Readers results will vary depending on a number of factors. Any and all claims or representations as to income earnings are not to be considered as average earnings. Testimonials are not representative. This book and all products and services are for educational and informational purposes only. Use caution and see the advice of qualified professionals. Check with your accountant, attorney or professional adviser before acting on this or any information. You agree that Diane Rolston is not responsible for the success or failure of your personal, business, health or financial decisions relating to any information presented by Diane Rolston, or company products/services. Earning potential is entirely dependent on the efforts, skills and application of the individual person.

Any examples, stories, references, or case studies are for illustrative purposes only and should not be interpreted as testimonies and/or examples of what reader and/or consumers, can generally expect from the information. No representation in any part of this information, materials and/or seminar training are guarantees or promises for actual performance. Any statements, strategies, concepts, techniques, exercise and ideas in the information materials and/or seminar training offered are simply opinion or experience, and thus should not be misinterpreted as promises, typical results or guarantees (expressed or implied). The author and publisher Diane Rolston or any of Diane Rolston's representatives shall in no way, under any circumstances be held liable to any party (or third party) for any direct, indirect, punitive, special, incidental or other consequential damages arising directly or indirectly from any use of books, materials and or seminar trainings which is provided "as is" and without warranties.

PRINTED IN CANADA

# Motivate, Inspire & Empower Those Around You with the Trailblazer Secrets!

PICK UP AND SHARE THIS BOOK AND THE REST OF THE SERIES WITH OTHERS

## Retail $29.95

### Special Quantity Discounts

|  |  |
|---|---|
| 5-20 Books | $21.95 |
| 21-99 Books | $18.95 |
| 100-499 Books | $15.95 |
| 500-999 Books | $10.95 |
| 1000+ Books | $8.95 |

### To Place and Order Contact:
(778)235.5819
team@dianerolston.com
dianerolston.com

# TABLE OF CONTENTS

| | |
|---|---|
| DEDICATION | 3 |
| WHAT OTHERS ARE SAYING | 4 |
| ACKNOWLEDGMENTS | 13 |
| A WELCOME MESSAGE TO YOU FROM DIANE | 14 |
| ABOUT THE PUBLISHER: DIANE ROLSTON | 18 |
| **Paula Kent** | 36 |
| **Aaron Turnbull-Holmes** | 38 |
| **Andrea Wyatt** | 40 |
| **Ashley Mckie** | 42 |
| **Barbara Wallick** | 44 |
| **Dr Barnsley Brown** | 46 |
| **Beck Barcy** | 48 |
| **Catherine Deluca** | 52 |
| **Charmaine Moules** | 54 |
| **Cindy MacCormack** | 56 |
| **Cora Naylor** | 58 |
| **Dana Zarcone** | 60 |
| **Debra Durma** | 62 |
| **Debra Rieder** | 64 |
| **Glynis E. Devine** | 66 |
| **Heide Baer** | 68 |
| **Janice Bannister** | 70 |
| **Jeanine Becker** | 74 |
| **Jo-Ann Wolloff** | 82 |

| | |
|---|---|
| Jodi Huettner | 84 |
| Karissa Ramos | 86 |
| Kathy Fester | 88 |
| Kendra Dahlstrom | 92 |
| Kimberly Lyall | 96 |
| Kristine Daruca | 100 |
| Leah Grant | 102 |
| Linda Hunt | 104 |
| Lorraine Peters | 106 |
| Marina Leung | 108 |
| Rai Hyde Cornell | 110 |
| Robyn Queen | 112 |
| Rochelle Odesser | 114 |
| Sally K. Norton | 116 |
| Sara and Rachel Nakamura | 118 |
| Sereda Fowlkes | 120 |
| Shannon Gander | 122 |
| Shelly Lynn Hughes | 124 |
| Susan Cumberland | 126 |
| Susan Fox Dixon | 128 |
| Susan Mielke | 130 |
| Tanya Steele | 132 |
| Tina Collura | 136 |
| | |
| ***BONUS MATERIAL*** | 139 |
| Diane Rolston Interviewed by Jack Canfield | 140 |
| What Stops Women from Blazing a Trail | 149 |
| One Final Message | 156 |

> "**Fill your cup** today to have **ENERGY** tomorrow."
>
> ~ Diane Rolston

# ACKNOWLEDGMENTS

I'd like to acknowledge my clients and the Dynamic Women® Global Club Members who have believed in the vision and mission of Dynamic Women®. You have been the reality to my dream, the fuel to my fire, and the reason why I do what I do.

I'm acknowledging all the authors: having so many of my Dynamic Women® members, clients and connections in this book has made it a complete joy to publish together. You are all wonderfully Dynamic Women!

Special thanks to my team Kristine Daruca, and Karissa Ramos, and editor Paula Kent for their support in bringing this book to life.

# A Welcome Message to You from Diane

**Hello there! I wanted to connect with you personally before you read this Book.**

You have made a wise decision to read this book. It is the 3rd in the series of Dynamic Women® Secrets books, with *Dynamic Women® Success Secrets* being the 1st and *Dynamic Women® Confidence Secrets* the 2nd. Whether you're already called a trailblazer or you feel like you need lots of growth in this area, you will learn, be inspired, and use the secrets to blaze more of a trail.

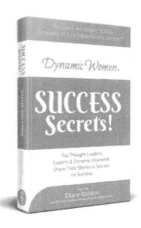

You will love hearing from so many incredible women. Many of whom are clients, colleagues, and friends of mine. You'll even hear from my two team members from the Philippines, Kristine and Karissa. Everyone has their view on what it takes to be a trailblazer in a particular area of life, in a unique situation or a specific industry.

When I coach my clients, lead Dynamic Women® events and speak to audiences, I see that so many women wish things could be different—that they could be different. I hear women yearning for being a trailblazer. It's not about changing yourself; it's more about focusing on the skills and expertise you have that you can grow and master to blaze a trail. This message is why I wanted to put together a book to bring you the stories and secrets from women on being a trailblazer. Dynamic Women are trailblazers in many ways. I should probably add it as a 10th pillar to the Program and Book called *Dynamic You*.

While *Trailblazer Secrets* is my 5th self-published book, *Dynamic You* was my first book. I wrote it because I found that not only do women want to do well in every area of life and every situation. They also wish they could step out of the day-to-day and into what they truly want and feel more self-assured about it. They aspire to belong in every place and every situation. They wish obstacles felt easier and smaller. That their goals felt within reach, and they wish they had a reliable system to pursue these things so that nothing would get in their way. Do you feel any of this?

It is why *Dynamic You* came to be. I've pieced together my experience in leading over 500 workshops from years of coaching, facilitating countless Dynamic Women® events, and numerous speaking engagements. I have collected the knowledge I have acquired from all the women I've met through my events and international coaching clients. I have compiled every bit of invaluable information, piecing it together into an 8-week program. The same program through which I have trained hundreds of other women.

The information in Dynamic You™ is the foundation on which I shifted my life. Since then, I've been living more as my full self and successfully realizing my goals. You can make the shift too! If you want to know more about the Pillars and the program, please go to dianerolston.com/dynamicyou.

Just like the *Dynamic You* book being a course, you have the opportunity to treat this book like a training program and apply what I am teaching, and the other authors are sharing. Even though I'm not leading you through group coaching, you will still gain knowledge, understanding and tools to become more of a trailblazer.

When I wondered what I should share as my contribution to the book, I kept returning to the trainings I created for the Trailblazer Summit I hosted which kicked off the idea of this collaborative book. Also, I'll be sharing one of my most recent passions: helping high level women to stop flying under the radar. Honestly, the fact that we have tall poppy syndrome, and that people will try to take down others because of their success makes me mad and so I am speaking up about it in this book.

If you prefer to listen to it, you can go here:
bit.ly/DW218Podcast
If you prefer to watch me talk about it, please go here:
bit.ly/DW218YouTube

Remember, the most successful and wealthiest people in the world read lots of books, so you are already on the right path by having this one in your hands. Now it is time to implement what you read about in the 42 secrets, my section and the bonus material that will help you year after year. *Dynamic Women® Trailblazer Secrets* holds the tools you need to enable a shift in your mindset. This shift will support your growth and ramp up what is possible, empowering you to achieve better results. I feel blessed that I get to impact others and inspire them, and I'm so grateful for every day that I get to continue to live this DYNAMIC life. And I'm thankful for people like you who choose to grow!

Stay Dynamic!

Diane Rolston
Award-Winning Coach
Speaker, Author, Podcaster
CEO & Founder of Dynamic Women®
Virtual Assistant Specialist
Wife & Mom of two

P.S. Here are 3 FREE opportunities to learn, grow and connect with Diane:

1. Grab your Free Gift and Diane Rolston's Website: FreeGiftFromDiane.com

2. Listen and be inspired on the Dynamic Women Podcast: https://podcasts.apple.com/us/podcast/id1467049886

3. Join free trainings, & connect with other Dynamic Women® in the FREE Facebook group: facebook.com/groups/DynamicWomenGlobalClub

P.P.S. Want to be an author in a future Dynamic Women® Secrets Book? Learn more here: dianerolston.com/be-an-author

# About the Publisher: Diane Rolston

is a leading authority in being a Dynamic Woman® and living a Dynamic Life. Combining a mix of coaching and personal development, Diane works with women to provide clarity, boost confidence and get them into action. She is a Certified Professional Coach, an International Speaker, Author, Workshop Leader and the CEO and Founder of Dynamic Women® Global Club and Podcast (a 5-Time Award Winning podcast in the top 2.5% podcasts). She was acknowledged as the Women of Worth "Motherpreneur of the Year" Award Winner, Top Mom Blogger in Vancouver, and Top 50 Mom Podcaster for her professional accomplishments and for the powerful impact she has on the women she inspires and empowers.

Diane left the life of the 9-5 employee and simultaneously became an entrepreneur and mother. Now a mother of two, business owner and community leader she considers herself an expert in change, work/life balance, prioritizing and getting things done! Diane's diverse work experience enables her to have a deeper understanding of what it takes to achieve our best and to live with more confidence and satisfaction. She believes we are not defined by our titles and our roles, instead we are more powerful and happy when we can be who we are. This brought out "Dynamic You", a book and a program, where she leads women to unleash the Dynamic Woman in them.

With her special mix of dynamics and heart she founded the group called, Dynamic Women®, where she facilitates engaging activities called "Coaching in Action" to help women get clear about their greatness, their success catalysts and the solutions to the obstacles (and all the while building strong relationships with other dynamic women). They meet and connect at live in person and virtual events.

Diane has presented at international women's business seminars, professional development conferences, in house for companies and on summits. She can speak to groups ranging from 10-10,000+. With clients across North America she has worked with non-profit executives, top management leaders, small business owners, and professional women helping them get better results in a shorter amount of time. She sees women sabotage themselves, get overwhelmed and second-guess their choices and uses her powerful questions to give clarity to what they really want and how they are going to achieve it. In 1:1 coaching sessions or one of her programs like "Dynamic Balance", she helps people break down big goals and build confidence so they can tackle their greatest obstacles, fears and reach more success.

Diane is a behind the scenes business advisor and coach for many business professionals, speakers, authors, thought leaders, and high achievers. Teaching anyone who wants to increase their results, how to correctly manage, package, and sell their time, experience, and expertise. Clients tell Diane that they love her sense of humor. That, "She's a positive person who constantly challenges your limits and helps you keep growing". Audiences comment on her dynamic style and how she always gives them a tool or challenge they can put into action and inspires them to make the changes they have been putting off.

Diane has leveraged her team of Virtual Assistants to help her to work less yet achieve more. She is now sharing her techniques in delegating and training her VAs, plus all the tools they use. In VA Made Easy, Diane hires your Dynamic Virtual Assistant for you and shows you a simple process to be able to maximize your VA's time. In addition, this program is designed to move you from task overwhelm to business ease and give you back time to focus on what matters most to you. You will learn what to delegate and how to easily train them to do it. Plus, you get so many of her Systems, Processes, Trainings, Strategy & Support.

In her own pursuits like playing soccer, hiking and doing stand-up, she pushes her limits, faces what scares her and loves to tackle a variety of projects. As a mother, wife, coach and business owner Diane acts with love and courage because she knows that in all parts of our life, we have the opportunity to inspire others. More than anything, she focuses on her goals in life and helps other women do the same.

*"I'm on a mission to have more women be unapologetically themselves and have the courage to step into the success they have always wanted." ~ Diane Rolston*

**Get all set at dianerolston.com for more clarity, confidence and action in your life and business.**

**Dynamic Women®** is an international community of success-oriented women who take action to develop skills, increase results and are focused on supporting each other to be DYNAMIC in every area of life! Our members get access to success coaching, additional online educational activities, and the invaluable networking connections they need to reach their personal or professional goals.

**Go to dynamicwomenclub.com to learn more and join the Global Club.**

Diane is the ideal speaker for your next conference or event. Email team@dianerolston.com to share about your speaker needs.

To see her in action, go to:
dianerolston.com/speaking
Connect with Diane on LinkedIn:
linkedin.com/in/dianercoaching
Connect with Diane personally on Facebook:
facebook.com/dianerolstoncoach
Connect with Diane professionally on Facebook:
facebook.com/LifeCoachDiane
Learn from Diane on YouTube:
youtube.com/c/CoachDianeRolston
Connect with Diane Rolston on Twitter:
https://twitter.com/DianeRCoaching
Diane Rolston on Instagram:
instagram.com/coachdianerolston/
Here what I'm up to and other opportunities here:
linktr.ee/dianerolston

# WHY WE'RE FOCUSING ON BEING A TRAILBLAZER
### By Diane Rolston

Being a trailblazer wasn't something I set out to do or someone I wanted to be. I had no association with the word until the beginning of my coaching journey as a client to my very first life coach.

Well over a decade ago, she had me do a values exercise for the first time. I knew things that were important to me, and I had set morals, but I lived by no locked-in values. I didn't realize this was a thing to do outside of a company's values. And I was so grateful to be able to do it.

One of my values that came up was leadership or being a leader. I've always felt that I've been a leader in school, on sports teams and clubs and even with friends; it just always comes up.

What I felt, though, was I had a negative response to the word leader because I don't like when someone acts like, "I am the leader, and you are my followers, and you need to do what I say." It had a negative feeling for me. It was taking power and freedom away from the individual. And when I redefined it, the word that came up instead was Trailblazer.

I love the idea of trailblazing because, in the true definition, it's when someone goes and blazes a trail on the trees, so you can then go back and show people the path, so even if you're not there, people can see where to go. I love applying that idea in coaching, running my women's communities, and my different work.

As a trailblazer, I go forward, I go ahead, to try things out, make mistakes and learn the fastest route to a goal or achievement. Then, I show you where to go by creating a clear path. I return to where you are and stand either beside you, in front of you or behind you. Whatever you need. I am with you as you then follow the steps easily.

It can be on so many topics and goals:
- How to build confidence
- How to work with a virtual assistant
- How to feel more balanced
- How to design a program/course
- How to create a life plan
- How to offer from the stage
- Or how to live with more resonance, which is what the values exercise did for me.

That is the idea of trailblazing, and there's so much more to it that I'll cover in the following sections, as well as giving examples from my own life so you can see the connection in yours. Also, I felt it was essential to share my thoughts and experiences with you, in addition to curating the stories and secrets of other female trailblazers who work in diverse industries to aid in your learning and understanding.

Before we jump into their secrets, I'll share more about what a trailblazer is and ways to know how you're being a trailblazer. I will also share why you may want to be a trailblazer or become more of a trailblazer. As you read this book, ask yourself, "Am I doing these things already? Do I need to bring these things in? Or do I need to increase the volume to get to the next level on each piece?

**What is a Trailblazer?**

If we look at the dictionary, there's another meaning to being a trailblazer: a pioneer or someone considered a first in their expertise. Or I guess you could say in whatever they're doing in their career, their passions, and the goals they're putting forward.

What I want to do here is for you to be able to think about how you're a trailblazer in your own life, in your career/business and in other areas. For example, maybe in your faith or your personal development, you're a trailblazer.

Since a trailblazer is a pioneer or someone considered a first in their area of expertise, they're willing to take risks and create a path that isn't already there. They blaze a trail and leave a path for others.

I like this definition rather than being a distant CEO, boss, or leader who's acting like I've done this, and I'm way up here, and you need to find me. A Trailblazer comes back to stand with you and shows you the way.

Here are some examples of how you can blaze a trail in your career and/or business:

| Area of life or topic | How do you blaze a trail? |
| --- | --- |
| Ex. 1: Investing | Example 1: Teaching others how to build wealth through passive crypto investing. |
| Ex. 2: Doctor | Example 2: Working on a new cure for a terrible disease. |
| Ex. 3: Speaker | Example 3: Using new technology in your speaking engagements to show up in person as a hologram when you're virtual. |

Ok some of these may be the cream of the industries. But you get the point.

Here are some examples from everyday life:

| Area of life or topic | How do you blaze a trail? |
|---|---|
| Ex. 1: Baking | Example 1: Creating gluten free, sugar free recipes that actually taste good. |
| Ex. 2: Triathlons | Example 2: Teaching how to compete in triathlons as a woman over 50 who works full time. |
| Ex. 3: Gardening | Example 3: Sharing about balcony produce gardens that can feed a family of four. |

Even if you're not making money off these areas of expertise and are just sharing and educating you are still impacting your local network or people online, so you can still be a trailblazer.

Now it's your turn. Where in your life do you excel and blaze a trail?

| Area of life or topic | How do you blaze a trail? |
|---|---|
|  |  |

-
-

If you haven't found where you're a trailblazer yet, then read the next section with the question of, where am I doing these five things?

# ARE YOU A TRAILBLAZER?

Now that I have you thinking about where you are already being a trailblazer, let's check these trailblazer clues to see if you are a trailblazer.

**Clue 1: Trailblazers are experts leading the way in their expertise so others can follow.**

There are two pieces to this. The first is, trailblazers are experts.

That's the first question for you is, what are you an expert in?

```
[                                                    ]
```

If you feel like you're a leader in your expertise, like you've mastered what you do, so that others can follow you, then you have a chance to be a trailblazer.

Second piece. Are you leading the way in your expertise? If so, how?

```
[                                                    ]
```

If not, how can you step up a little bit more?

```
[                                                    ]
```

## Clue 2: Trailblazers are leaders who point the way

They need a vision to be able to point others to the way right to go. So are you considering yourself as a leader?

- *Where do you lead?*
- *Do you point the way to others?*
- *Do you show the way to others?*

|  |
|---|
|  |

They're also leaders who point the way because they have a vision.

What vision or mission do you have, or movement are you creating?

- *Do you share your vision?*
- *Do you have a clear vision?*

|  |
|---|
|  |

There are lots of questions here. And if you're starting to think there are so many questions, I don't think I can go through them all right now. That's okay.

**Clue 3: Trailblazers are determined, so obstacles can't stop them.**

Obstacles are tricky, right? We all have this feeling of, oh my goodness, this is scary, or I'm fearful. Will this work? We all face obstacles, but the thing is, trailblazers have the courage to face them, and then they have the determination to get past any obstacles or roadblocks that stop them. They sidestep; they keep going. They persevere.

So I ask you, *Do you know what's stopping you?*
*How much are you letting those things stop you?*
*Do you have the courage to face the things that you're fearful of that are holding you back?*

The great thing about trailblazers is that you might not know how to do something, but you do it anyway. And when you do that and have courage, others will feel like, *"Wow, that's such an inspiration; I can learn from her."*

**Clue 4: Trailblazers can unite with people from all different industries.**

When they get into collaboration and community with others, they flourish. There's that excitement of, I'm blazing a trail over here, and you're blazing a trail over there. And then when we come together, we can flourish together, we can thrive together, because we're doing so well in our industries, in our paths that we get to speak that same language.

Trailblazers do not feel that they compete with others; they prefer to work together to make their vision a reality.

How do you collaborate with others?
What do you wish you could collaborate on?
Who do you wish you could unite with?

### Clue 5: Trailblazers are always learning

They're growing in wisdom in their field, in mastery of their skills. Trailblazers are always curious, asking, how can I learn? How can I get better? Curiosity is an excellent quality to apply to all life areas.

Then, they apply the fantastic technology that's out there. I know that you've probably been able to move forward with your goals or even in areas of your health because of technology supporting that growth.

So these are the five top clues if you are a trailblazer. Are you one? Can you be more of one?

If you feel you are a trailblazer, you'll read the next section with the question, how well am I doing each of these five things?

# THE FIVE MYTHS YOU'VE BEEN LED TO BELIEVE

Now let's dive in here to the five myths you've been led to believe by others that are causing you not to get the desired results while making you feel overwhelmed and overworked.

**Myth number one:** It takes <u>a lot of time</u> to make changes.

That is a myth. Why is it a myth?

It takes <u>the right strategy</u> to make significant changes.

This first myth reminds me of Jacquie, who was able to take a three-year goal and scrunch it into two main steps. Through coaching, she got clarity and could see the right strategy to achieve her goal. She felt confident and achieved the first step in just 30 days and the other in six months. The first step was her buying an RV, and the second was prepping her house for sale, selling it, and achieving her goal of a nomadic lifestyle. It's pretty amazing how she reached her dream so quickly. And it was based on the right strategy and taking action.

**Myth number two**: I wasn't born a leader, a trailblazer, or confident. Therefore, <u>it doesn't come naturally, so I can't do it</u>.

I hear that all the time. Maybe you're saying other things like I'm too old, my weight isn't where I want it to be. I'm sick. I'm not as pretty. I'm not like my other friends. I'm not calm. I'm not these things, so it will take a lot of work; I can't do it.

It doesn't matter if it doesn't come naturally; you can <u>put steps into place to improve that area or focus on your current strengths</u>.

The first part of the transformation is the awareness of where you are currently. For example, you feel, *"I'm not that confident."* Okay, so let's implement a plan to be more confident.

**Myth number three:** I don't need help. <u>I know what to do</u>.

I'm sure you've heard this from people in your life, or you've been guilty of it yourself. It's great that you know what to do, but are you doing it?

Have you been in that situation? You know that you need to put in a specific structure for something, but you're just not doing it? You know you'll eat better when you meal plan, but you're not meal planning. You know you may go if you put your clothes out for the gym. So you know a lot of things, but you're not implementing them.

It's not enough to know something; <u>you need to implement it or take steps towards it</u>. To take those steps could mean you need someone to show you, help you and keep you accountable.

Clients who got help to implement were able to land more clients, publish a book, launch a course, get their dream job, lose weight, find their dream partner, and so many more things.

**Myth number four:** <u>It's too expensive</u> to invest in yourself.

Maybe you invest in a coach, or you invest in courses, or you do some personality tests. The fact is, <u>it's costly to not invest in yourself</u>.

I have a few coaches and people on my uplevel team. They're each for different areas of my life and different purposes. I've saved so much time, energy, stress and money by making the right decisions with their coaching, getting the best feedback, and having the advice when I needed it the most.

Over the years, even with just one of my coaches, I've probably invested over $100,000 in his fee, flying to meet him, meals, and accommodation. But I know without him and the others; I wouldn't be where I am today, doing the cool things I'm grateful to do and making the money I'm blessed to have earned. I'm always looking for a 10x ROI (Return on Investment). I hope you will see your ROI when you invest in yourself.

**Myth number five:** I don't care about the money. I want to help more people.

This myth is hurting so many people. Saying, "I'm not here to make money." Often shows up in the actions of discounting, not charging or offering free beta opportunities.

I understand you want to impact more people. BUT if you're going to have a huge impact, you must give some focus to the money.

It's not about giving money all the power or being greedy. Here are some things that my clients have been able to do when they give more attention to the money side of their business:
- They gave more to their community,
- They created a better life for themselves and their family.
- They doubled their ticket sales and donated more to charity.
- They retired their spouse from a draining job.
- They had time off to volunteer.
- They could build scholarships into their programs.

When you make an abundance (whatever that means to you), you can step more into giving. This has helped me donate more to women's shelters, which is important to me. Whether I donate books or money, I strive to support and meet women's shelter needs, specifically at the time. Giving more focus on the money has also helped me to be more generous with my clients and even better at what I do.

So, that was the five myths and their solutions. Which do you want to place your attention on?

_____

I congratulate you on completing this section. I know you will get so much out of the rest of the book. When you read take notes, implement the learning and check out each author's links and profiles.

Stay Dynamic!
~ Diane

"HAVE THE **COURAGE** TO **STEP INTO** THE **SUCCESS** YOU HAVE ALWAYS WANTED"

~ Diane Rolston

# NOW BEGINS THE CONTRIBUTIONS
## FROM TOP THOUGHT LEADERS, EXPERTS & DYNAMIC WOMEN®!

The accomplished entrepreneurs and professionals were selected for the book because of their commitment to serving others and willingness to share their secrets for being a Trailblazer.

The authors' pieces are shared in alphabetical order by 1st name, except for the editor Paula Kent, as her piece felt like such a powerful way to start this collaborative book.

You get to choose how to read them: All in one sitting. One Trailblazer Secret a day or One Trailblazer Secret a week. With 42 contributors and the Trailblazer Training by Diane Rolston, doing one a week works well because it gives you time to implement the learning, but in the end it's all up to you.

Just get started!

# TRAILBLAZER SECRET #1
## The Sisterhood of Determination
*Paula Kent*

She stands upon a trail, staring not down the path but to the side, into the darkness, pausing as she considers a new way forward. As she stands, she feels a murmur, a slight vibration, a tingling awareness of connection—awareness blooms, and she embodies the life-giving energy of our ancient earth: scared but courageous, timid, and yet empowered.

She stands and breathes; her breath holds within itself the breath of the elders who have walked before. Those devalued, pushed aside, dismissed, mocked, and persecuted. Our Elders, whom history has named Witch, Crone, Hag, and only occasionally Wise. Names are dependent upon the whim of those who judge.

She stands and thinks. She holds within her cells the ancient wisdom that she is enough. She is steadfast in self-belief that the murmur within is the voice of her soul.

She acts! In her first step, the plan emerges; she is aware of the obstacles and acknowledges that the challenges she cannot see hold grave danger. She carves a new path; regardless of feeling ready, she pushes forward. It is messy, hurts, and punishes; the trail makes no promises.

She pauses; she stands powerful upon her path, passionately believing that she can unlock the promise of her soul. As she blazes the trail, she adds her voice, spirit, and soul to sing harmoniously, to mix with our existence's magic and meaning. She moves forward once again, crafting a trail into the beyond.

Who is she? She has lived before us, and she is yet to be born. She is me, and she is you.

---

**Paula Kent** is a lifelong learner researching gendered ageism while pursuing a Doctorate in Social Sciences. In addition to her research, Paula is an award-winning writer. Her first book, Heroic Choices: The Inner Journey of Transformation, is a Goody Business Award Finalist. Heroic Choices examines the critical phases of personal change, positioning fear and failure as positive directives essential to transforming oneself into one's soul purpose. Paula is developing a modern fairy tale exploring female aging as an aspirational action. Paula is honoured once again to participate in the Dynamic Women Secrets Series.

Email: pjkent@telus.net
LinkedIn: @paulajkent
Website: paulakent.com

# TRAILBLAZER SECRET #2
## A Mother's Tale of Home Business Success
### *Aaron Turnbull-Holmes*

Looking back 26 years to the birth of my first child, I knew I couldn't commit to a traditional 9-5 job from the first moment I saw him. So began my journey of finding and working in creative ways to earn a living while raising my son.

Fast forward 11 years now, holding my daughter, understanding my need to find work that allowed for quality time with her as she grew.

With a supportive husband (who refers to me as his "Swiss Army Wife") behind me, I made the first step into my new reality built around the skill I had been teaching myself – cake decorating, much like you see on TV competitions. Despite not having a shop front, I was slowly building a customer base that contributed to the household income without sacrificing time with my kids.

I say kids because it was at this time, I also decided to take on the role of schooling my oldest at home. It sounds nuts - and maybe a little bonkers, but I was up for the challenge.

Skip ahead another four years, and with it came the realization of the importance of an online presence for a thriving business. So, I began a new venture to learn how to promote myself effectively online.

This journey ignited a newfound passion for creating digital content and building a community around my work. Inspired by my love for this new avenue of creativity, I fully immersed myself in the digital realm, assisting others in creating, editing, and promoting their work.

Jump ahead another ten years to the present day, and here you will find me homeschooling my youngest (currently in grade 10) while working from home as a video and audio editor for multiple podcasts, managing multiple YouTube channels, and creating content for promotional use on platforms like Instagram, Facebook, and Pinterest.

Today, I am eager to share my passion for working from home with others, from young people transitioning out of school to stay-at-home parents seeking another income stream. My dream of balancing quality time with my children and flexible work hours is a secret I aim to share and help others achieve.

---

**Aaron Turnbull-Holmes** is a multifaceted content creator, audio-video editor, writer, and homeschooling mother of two. She is sharing her journey to empower yours.

Facebook: @creativityatsayitwith
Instagram: @sayitwith.ca
Website: sayitwith.ca

# TRAILBLAZER SECRET #3
## A Mother's Trailblaze from Adversity to Entrepreneurial Triumph
*Andrea Wyatt*

In the pages of my life, I share a transformative narrative that has shaped me into who I am today. This story isn't just about a woman's journey; it's about my journey – one defined by resilience, transformation, and the pursuit of dreams against all odds.

Emerging from an abusive relationship shattered my self-confidence and eroded my self-worth. But courage led me away from that darkness, clutching onto the strength deep within, propelling me to trailblaze the path I stand on today.

1. Rediscovering Self-Worth - My children's eyes reflected my potential, a potent reminder that I was more than my past. Through introspection, I reignited passions and talents buried within me.

2. The Strength of Support - I didn't walk this path alone, nor should any of us. An incredible network of friends, family, and mentors surrounded me. Their unwavering belief fueled my determination to rise above my history, becoming the bedrock on which, I rebuilt my life.

3. Never Stop Learning - I am committed to personal and professional growth from adversity's ashes. I invested in myself through reading, coaching, and attending events that enriched my knowledge and skills.

4. Entrepreneurial Journey - My journey took a new turn as I embraced entrepreneurship. A supportive business partner believed in me, and we crafted a platform to impact lives

together. Simultaneously, I launched another business aiding insurance agency owners in managing social media and marketing needs.

As I recount my voyage, I extend an invitation to draw inspiration from my tale. My accomplishments stand as tangible proof that scars don't define us. It's our resilience that molds us into architects of our destinies.

---

**Andrea Wyatt,** the Program Director of The Unstoppable Profit Producer Program, is also the Founder/Owner of Marketing Insurance Solutions. Andrea leads our exceptional team, lending her unparalleled expertise in computers, websites, Excel, and Microsoft. A true powerhouse behind the scenes, she ensures coaching members receive top-  notch tools and resources. Hailing from Sentinel, Oklahoma, GO OU, Andrea's passion for community shines through her charity work, complementing her role as a devoted mother of two boys. With a heart for impact, she's making history since her leap into entrepreneurship in 2013.

LinkedIn: @andreawyatt
Website: unstoppableprofitproducer.com

# TRAILBLAZER SECRET #4
## Clear is Kind - Giving People the Feedback They Need to Succeed
*Ashley Mckie*

I prepared for a difficult conversation. I reviewed my notes and highlighted specific examples of my concerns, then braced myself to be uncomfortable because I had a team member, I wasn't confident I could develop. One well-intentioned, tough conversation completely changed the course. This team member had held similar jobs and lacked confidence, knowing something was not quite right but never told what. Our conversation ended with her saying, "No one ever told me that." An 'ah-ha' moment which catalyzed her transformation into a valuable top performer. By providing specific feedback, delivering it with compassion, and embracing her coachability, we went from failing to thriving. This conversation didn't change everything overnight, but it opened the door to deeper trust and better communication, essential to successful relationships.

In a time when succession planning is top of mind - mastering the skill of attracting and retaining top talent is critically important. Giving people the information that they need to grow quickly is imperative. Preparing those around you to sprint down the leadership trail you blazed faster and more easily is a competitive advantage. People learn best by doing but they also want to know if they are veering off course. Increase your team's effectiveness by being transparent with expectations, performance evaluation, and, most importantly, meaningful praise. Saying "great job" doesn't help anyone identify what tool they have just added to their belt; being clear about what is working and what isn't improves confidence, reduces anxiety, and allows those you influence to use that information to their benefit. Similarly, hiding constructive feedback with excessive positivity or superficiality can confuse or lose the intended message. Providing feedback may be one of the trickiest parts of leadership, but with preparation, good intentions and some simple tips and tricks, it can become one of the most significant rewards of your career.

---

**Ashley Mckie** is a Canadian Registered Safety Professional and Certified Health and Safety Consultant. Recognized as one of Canada's Top Women in Safety in 2023 for her contributions to safety leadership. As a Director of Safety, she effortlessly merges expertise with her vibrant personality in her relentless pursuit of continuous improvement. Whether on podcasts or speaking with teams, Ashley thrives in sharing insights with diverse audiences. Beyond her professional achievements, she is an active volunteer, shaping her personal and professional communities.

LinkedIn: @ashley-mckie-crsp-chsc

# TRAILBLAZER SECRET #5
## Going from Stressed to Blessed
### *Barbara Wallick*

Do you know what it's like to be still?

Today, most women wear multiple hats; we are the caretakers, troubleshooters and the glue that holds everything together—leaving little time or energy for our self-care. In 2021, my 50-year-old brother died of a stroke & brain bleed. I felt furious at him; what a waste of life! So much emotion raged through me. I just wanted to strike out, smash something or hurt myself physically.

Once I calmed down, I realized this was my wake-up call. It was time to check myself out. To my horror, my test results showed that my Heart was aging much faster than my body. I was 57 at the time, yet my heart age was 80. I thought I was taking care of myself.

What was I missing? I discovered that being in a constant state of elevated STRESS was the cause.

YES! STRESS - the slow, silent Killer. I had been dealing with a lot of stress! A high-stress career and illness in my family, amongst other things, was silently wearing me out, even though it wasn't visible from the outside.

I felt proud, thinking I handled my stress well. Discovering this saved my life. As I explored this deeply, I realized I was ADDICTED to STRESS! I was known as the "FIXER," the go-to person to solve problems in all areas of my life. Putting out fires turned me on, and I felt lost without them.

Today, I've moved from Stressed to Blessed through deep self-enquiry, mindfulness, and meditation. I've learned to align my Body, Mind, and spirit with nature's rhythm, a lifelong practice I fully embrace.

My life's path is to Heal and live in Harmony while embracing daily stress. My mission is to teach Women to embrace self-care so they, too, feel at peace while enjoying life's abundance despite daily stress.

---

**Barbara Wallick** has a lifetime of experiences to share with her clients. Working in one of the most highly stressed industries, "Finance," she has learned to be a Trailblazer in her healing journey, teaching Women that success is learning how to be Healthy in a Stress-filled World.

Barbara is a Master NLP Coach/Hypnotherapist and wellness advocate for Women who are feeling the stress of life & want to learn how to Heal in Mind, Body, and spirit.

Facebook: @barb.wallick
Instagram: @barbaraswallick
Website: barbwallick.com

# TRAILBLAZER SECRET #6
## Do the Dang Thing Now!
### *Dr Barnsley Brown*

'Do the dang thing now!' Those are the words I heard one week after we went into lockdown in March 2021. With COVID raging, many people felt afraid, and I wanted to help. I was meditating when I heard, 'Start that Mastermind you've thought about for a decade, Barnsley; the time is NOW.'

I was no stranger to messages from Spirit that catapulted me out of my comfort zone. Over 20 years earlier, I followed my guidance and left academia to start my own business with no backup plan or second income, just one thousand bucks and a big dream.

I was done muting and 'academicizing' my voice to fit in. I longed to be fully self-expressed and fulfill my real calling. I wanted to integrate all of myself—mystic and marketer, speaker and writer, trailblazer, and coach/mentor—into a business. And I wanted to show others how to do the same.

On a given day, I may present a creative marketing seminar to business owners or train them to relieve stress and overwhelm using Reiki. I may coach my private clients in the mindset hacks and systems they need to reach six figures and beyond in the Mastermind program I finally created during lockdown. None of my gifts, education, and expertise fall by the wayside now.

How about you? Are you fully expressed in your work? Do you have a business you dream about yet never really begin? Or have you started that business but are not making the money/impact you want, so you are considering returning to a job you hate? Have you imprisoned yourself in someone else's vision of what your life and work should be?

When my Mastermind clients progress from making little to nothing at the beginning to enjoying $5k, $10k, or more months, they banish the naysayers in their heads and experience the juiciness of their passionate purpose. Together, we banish the words 'Someday I will...' from their lives.

How would it feel to be free from the prison of your 'Someday I will...'? You matter. Your contribution matters. You have a voice and a calling that is yours alone. It is time to listen and do the dang thing NOW!

---

**Dr. Barnsley Brown** helps big-hearted business owners reach six figures and beyond in her business presentations, Reiki training, and Make It Happen Mastermind. She has helped thousands in five countries over the past three decades. On weekends, you will find her performing improv and relaxing with her daughter and their rescue animals.

LinkedIn: @kickasscoachingandreiki
Website: spirited-solutions.com
YouTube: @drbarnsleync

# TRAILBLAZER SECRET #7
## "You Think You Have Time" Buddha
### *Beck Barcy*

For two decades, I have run a non-medical home care company that matches Caregivers with Clients wherever they call home. Our clients are typically 80-105 years young. I love to learn from their wisdom and share it. I found a common thread to their advice and Buddha's quote, "You think you have time."

Stories that bring a glow to their faces are the ones of the chances they took going against the grain, struggles they survived when they thought they either mentally or physically couldn't, and the focus and the strength they found in overcoming challenges. It didn't always matter if they were 100% successful. Some were highly emotional journeys, but they stayed the course. Doing what you say and keeping your word to others, but also yourself, is always a high priority, as well.

These are stories of perseverance, strong values, faith and gratitude in appreciating even the struggle. Tales of a well-lived life also contributed to consistency and work ethic. Like this version of a short story: "The reporter asked the writer if he writes when inspired, and he responded, "Yes, and that is scheduled every day starting at 9 am." (Unknown)

Time is the most valuable asset anyone has. After decades of experience in the aging industry, it has become evident that what we spend our time on daily is directly linked to our quality of life.

We can't get back time we squander. For example, we waste precious hours if we allow gossip and complaining. 5% of 24 hours is 72 minutes a day/8 hours and 40 minutes a week/or 438 hours a year. 5% is a pretty low estimate, too! 10% is 876 hours a year wasted!

Decades will pass if you do not stop the world and block off time to do what could change your life. Strictly block time as if you were in a dentist's chair when no one could talk to you. Dust off life-altering projects, form new habits and get inspired. Do it daily, without interruptions, and be a finisher. It all starts with how we think, plan our time and imagine how it will feel. Buddha also said, "All that we are is a result of what we have thought about."

A final piece of advice I have learned is the importance of healthy eating. Pay serious attention to knowing your body's nourishment needs. For example, if we eat high histamine foods, we suffer itching, sneezing, puffy red, itchy eyes, scratching and even rashes that contribute to inflammation. You can't have disease without inflammation. Yet we keep eating foods that drain our energy and ignore those signs that happen right after we eat what our body is rejecting. Low histamine foods include blueberries, carrots, and grapes, but high histamine foods include tomatoes, strawberries, spinach, and almonds." Inflammation also creates weight we can't lose.

If you are not feeling Amazing every day, you have excuses to escape success daily. Investing your time in your health now is the only way I know how to gain more time. Sometimes decades!

For two decades, **Beck Barcy** has been the serial entrepreneur, CEO and CSA -Certified Senior Advisor for I Need An Angel Inc., a non-medical homecare company, High Fives Charity, a Non-Profit that "advocates for Seniors and those that care for them" in Scottsdale, AZ as well as pursuing a brand new journey on an off the grid property  learning and teaching sustainable living and mindset called Over The River Through The Woods LLC. in Belfast NY.

Email: hello@ineedanangel.com
Facebook: @INeedAnAngelInc and @Rbarcy

# "WHO YOU ARE MATTERS MORE THAN WHAT YOU DO."

~ DIANE ROLSTON

# TRAILBLAZER SECRET #8
## Being Change Resilient
## Not Change Resistant
### *Catherine Deluca*

How did a training session at work lead to my journey to change resiliency? After many changes in my life from childhood to adulthood, my reaction to a change was resistance, and the consequence was that I created chaos in my life and those around me.

Being trained in organizational change management and incorporating those strategies into my work made me realize that it is possible to break the resistance cycle and successfully manage change.

I discovered four critical skills that help build resiliency:

1. Trust that you know what you need.
2. Believe that no one is trying to sabotage you or to set you up to fail.
3. Acknowledge that life sometimes takes an unexpected path, but you control your reaction.
4. Faith that today might not be how you want it to be, but you can craft how you choose to navigate the way forward.

When faced with decisions, I learned that working through them helps to uncover the source of resistance and turn those into strengths. For myself, the turning point came during COVID. I was isolated in my home and from my family on the other side of the country and facing Christmas alone. Moving back to my home province had been something for the future. Still, I journaled on the four skills facing Christmas without family and the prospect of many more months of possible isolation. I created a summary of one statement for each. I knew I could rely on the truth of those statements, so the decision was easy. Most people in my life celebrated with me, some didn't, but I was confident that the decision to move was best for me.

My life now isn't perfect, but it is pretty amazing. It worked for me; it can work for you too!

---

**Catherine Deluca** works extensively with people and organizations, helping to navigate change. She is creative and passionate that change can be positive and that there is always a path to resiliency over resistance. She makes daily choices about what will bring her personal and professional satisfaction and believes everyone can have the life they want! She lives in rural Nova Scotia (not hard to find!) and enjoys small-town life, fresh air, and many walks with Bentley, her one-year-old daschund! Ask her about the top 10 things she learned from him about resiliency!

Email: cathy@deluca-co.com
Facebook: @Cathy.DelucaAndCo
LinkedIn: @cathy-deluca

# TRAILBLAZER SECRET #9
## Believing in Yourself and Overcoming Challenges
*Charmaine Moules*

I was 25, newly married, in a new house, and my adult life was beginning. I came home from work; my (then) husband prepared a beautiful meal for us and happily placed it on the table before me, looking very pleased with himself. We sat down to eat. I took a couple of bites, and he looked at me and said, "How is it?" I burst into tears. In his French accent, he said, "What can I do? More salt? I'll make you something else." I told him it wasn't about the food; that was perfect.

I hadn't told him I had been struggling at work; a female manager had bullied me for months. I was newly promoted to a team leader position, the youngest on my team and boss now to people who were my peers. Totally out of my comfort zone, I took on this new position and the challenge. I knew I could succeed; however, someone had a different view: a female manager who was my superior. She would get me into a room, close the door and bully me, verbally and many times leaning so far across the table that she was in my face or pounding her fists. Twenty-five years later, I can still picture her flaring nostrils, beady eyes, and red face and the sense of satisfaction she got from asserting her power over me.

At 27, I started my own business, Visions to Performance. I had a website in 2000 when most people didn't know the difference between a website and an email address. I didn't come from an entrepreneurial family, so there was so much uncertainty. Today, 23 years later, V2P is still running strong. How? I had faith I'd figure things out.

When faced with challenges, which voice is louder - trust or doubt? Do you rely on analysis (your head) or your emotional knowing (your gut) when making decisions?

I hope my story encourages you to believe and trust in yourself and know that you'll always find your way. Have faith in yourself, be resourceful and use your intuition alongside your analysis.

---

**Charmaine Moules** is an Executive Coach, Consultant, and Speaker who works with Leaders and teams in Fortune 100 companies globally. Her sweet spots are creating more emotionally intelligent workplaces, developing Leaders as Coaches, and creating connections with teams through relationship-focused conversations.

Email: charmaine@v2p.ca
LinkedIn: @Charmaine-Moules
Website: v2p.ca

# TRAILBLAZER SECRET #10
## Unlocking Your Potential
## by Shifting Perspective
### Cindy MacCormack

As a teen success coach, corporate leader, and mom, I've faced numerous challenges on my life journey. In those moments, one quote has been my guiding light, offering me a profound mindset shift to navigate life's hurdles and unlock my full potential. And I want to share it with you.

A quote often attributed to Buddha guides me: "If you focus on the hurt, you'll continue to suffer. If you focus on the lesson, you'll continue to grow." Its impact on my life has been profound, and I believe it's a message that everyone should hear.

Think about the last time something went wrong in your life. Maybe you got stuck in traffic, missed a social event, or faced a challenging assignment. We naturally ask ourselves, "Why is this happening to me?" We often get caught up in self-pity and negativity, letting setbacks define us.

But what if we shift our perspective? What if we see every setback as a lesson rather than an obstacle? Imagine the positive impact it could have on our lives. It all boils down to perspective. We limit ourselves to a cycle of suffering when we dwell on the negative. However, by shifting our focus to the positive, we unveil a world of possibilities for personal development and progress. I know it's not always easy, but it's worth it.

That is why I find mindset to be so powerful in my work with teens, and I guide them to embrace this empowering perspective. With adolescence comes challenges that require resilience and a positive mindset. This quote becomes their beacon of strength when faced with setbacks or disappointments. So, as I remind the teens I work with, the next time life throws you a curveball, choose to see it as an opportunity. Challenges occur for you, not to you. Even in moments of disappointment, valuable lessons are waiting to be discovered.

Embrace a positive mindset, keep your head high, and watch yourself grow in ways you never thought possible.

---

**Cindy MacCormack,** a certified teen success coach with over 15 years of wellness & corporate expertise, is on a mission to empower youth for success. She offers a unique real-world perspective as a proud mom of two remarkable teens. Her approach combines mindset, personal growth, and empowerment tools to unlock your teen's potential, boosting their confidence and resilience for lifelong success.

Instagram: @cindylmaccormack
LinkedIn: @cindymaccormackcoaching
Website: cindymaccormackcoaching.com

# TRAILBLAZER SECRET #11
## Start Your Journey from Within
### *Cora Naylor*

Do you ever feel like you're doing everything you should be but not getting the results or success you were hoping for? That's how I thought for a lot of my life. I always wondered what held me back or why I wasn't as successful as others.

I read all the books and did all the training. I could make a living out of learning. However, I never found the lasting success I was hoping for. It didn't stop me from trying, though!

It took a long time to realize that the reason I wasn't achieving what I was hoping for wasn't because I needed to learn more (it's easy to go there!).

I needed to step back and take a look inside myself—taking time to look at what I had done, where I was and where I wanted to go and not doubt myself and explore my capabilities. This included releasing a lot of "emotional baggage" holding me back.

You don't always realize that emotions cause your issues until you release them. Accompanying this release and slowing down can create fantastic change within. I'll admit that I'm not always good at slowing down. I'm still working on this practice. I fill my days keeping busy doing things - maybe that's just an avoidance method? Can you relate? The cool thing is that when I take the time to slow down and look at what I want rather than what I think I should be doing - the answers come. Allowing that space to think, to daydream again - giving that room - allows so many beautiful ideas to bloom. Do I still have days where I doubt myself and what I'm doing? I do. However,

I now have the tools to help me move forward to create the success and life I desire.

---

**Cora Naylor** is a Certified Emotion Code and Global Energy Method Practitioner, Life Coach and Podcast Host.

Cora is a lifelong learner, always looking for ways to improve herself. After working with an Emotion Code Practitioner, she found her "emotional baggage" was a big part which held her back. Once she "cracked the code" of her emotions, she knew she could help other women do the same using her energy-releasing processes.

Facebook: @cora.naylor
Instagram: @naylorcora
Website: coranaylor.com

# TRAILBLAZER SECRET #12
## Finding Your Authentic Swing
*Dana Zarcone*

By societal standards, I was successful! I climbed the corporate ladder, becoming a Vice President of a Fortune 100 company. I had an adoring husband, two beautiful daughters and a yacht. Yet, beneath this shimmering exterior, my soul was in turmoil with a deep-rooted dissonance gnawing at me. My life was more pretense than purpose. My personal power lay dormant. My soul was starving for something more authentic and more fulfilling.

One raw night, in the dim confines of my bathroom, Whitney Houston's "I Look to You" echoed as I wept. I was at rock bottom, feeling disconnected from my true self. I was exhausted from living a life devoid of my true passion and purpose.

It was time for a change. So, I left the corporate world and ventured into entrepreneurship. The transition was brutal—far from the fantasy of being my own boss in a frictionless universe. I burned through coaches and courses, sinking deeper into debt, emulating the formulas of those who appeared more successful. But the 'allness' of me—the unique essence only I could bring to the world—remained untapped.

Ultimately, the game-changer wasn't the next coach or course but believing in myself enough to step into my power and be the leader I was born to be. By tapping into the 'allness' of me, I discovered genuine happiness and success.

Today, my achievements aren't just markers on a resumé—they're milestones of my authentic journey. I've learned that your authentic swing, as Bagger Vance says, can't be taught - it must be discovered from within. You aren't just a complex cocktail of other people's expectations and societal norms. You are a unique soul bursting with the potential to effect real, lasting change and leave a legacy.

Helping others tap into their full potential has become my life's mission. We each have an intrinsic melody, a rhythm that's only ours, waiting to be played out loud.

Don't be swayed by the world's tune. Instead, dance to your own. The world doesn't need another echo; it yearns for your genuine voice. The path to true fulfillment is not in being a version of someone else but the most authentic version of you.

---

**Dana Zarcone** is a 6X #1 international bestselling author, a highly sought-after publisher, business coach, motivational speaker, and podcast host. Dana's gift is helping clients turn their passion and expertise into a best-selling book and successful business online.

Facebook: @DanaZarconeIntl
Instagram: @dana_zarcone
LinkedIn: @danazarcone

# TRAILBLAZER SECRET #13
## From Despair to Success:
## One School's Story
### *Debra Durma*

Jones Elementary School* was in deep trouble. The principal was passionate, energetic, and well-intentioned but had serious problems: underperforming school labels, student behavior issues, and low teacher motivation. 95% of students were on free and reduced lunch, and 42% were learning a new language. All these factors caused stress reflected in poor standardized test scores, the key metric to label schools.

How many of you know teachers and principals who feel these same stresses? When placing high demands on schools to improve failing scores, blaming, and complaining become part of the environment. Why? It's a natural tendency in a high-pressure atmosphere, but I believe it's avoidable. Teachers and leaders don't know what else to do. They lack clearly defined steps toward meaningful change.

That's where I come in: to help principals bridge the gap between dysfunction and despair to impact and performance. When I stepped in to help the principal at Jones Elementary, we put into place my proprietary "DATA" model for transforming her results: Define, Analyze, Transform, and Achieve.

We analyzed the root causes for the low-test scores and discovered a fundamental stumbling block: teachers felt beat up by data. The first step was to change mindsets and beliefs about using test scores. Empowering the principal to focus on the specific changes, clearly communicate expectations to staff, and create meaningful support for achieving better results.

Within three years, the school went from 34% of students reading at grade level to 59%. Energized by a new connection with data and coaching support, this principal, along with her staff, succeeded in blazing a new trail to success despite the significant obstacles they faced.

*School name is fictionalized; principal and schools' results are real.

---

**Debra Durma** is the Founder of STAR Leadership Systems, LLC, a data-driven company helping school leaders improve results. Debra leverages over 37 years of experience to catapult her clients toward success.

She has been a teacher, principal, district-level administrator, and national leadership consultant for the Center for Data Driven Reform (grant with John Hopkins University) and currently works with public, charter, and private schools. Debra is leading a movement to empower school leaders to change their results using data and leadership solutions.

If you know a school leader looking for answers, encourage them to contact Debra today.

Email: support@debradurma.com
LinkedIn: @debra-durma
Website: debradurma.com

# TRAILBLAZER SECRET #14
## Overcome Depression and Negative Thoughts
*Debra Rieder*

"I want out!" he said. My entire identity as wife and mother changed with those three words. I thought I would be stronger, but I wasn't. I crumbled. I slipped into depression but didn't realize it because the perfectionist in me still wore the daily "mask" and functioned properly.

Depression can be clinical or situational. These two are very different. Clinical depression is medically diagnosed and can be chronic, lasting for years. Situational depression is brought on in direct response to a situation(s) in life and is usually shorter in the length of time experienced but can be more intense.

I always share this information when speaking on stage or working with clients. Despite what you might think, situational depression does NOT come to you. You "go get it" ...almost as if you yell, "HEY DEPRESSION, HERE I AM!"

When you lie in bed or stay curled in a ball on the shower floor for hours, you're putting out the welcome mat for depression and writing out party invitations for self-deprecation and negative thoughts to play havoc with your mind. That's what I mean by "going to get depression."

Have you ever seen someone crying hysterically or hating themselves and their life while jogging on the treadmill, singing and jamming to their favorite song, watching a comedy show, or shopping in the mall? The answer is no.

I am not saying that you'll be instantly happy if you do these activities or similar ones. That's unrealistic. But I am saying if you minimize the welcome mat and party invitations and instead choose to do something active or physical, not allowing the rumination of negative thoughts to play mayhem in your mind, you can get out of situational depression more easily.

Trust me, I understand you may not "feel" like going out in public or getting out of bed...Do it anyway! Don't listen to your feelings. Your "feelings" will keep you trapped on the merry-go-round of suffering. In the words of Dalai Lama, "Pain is inevitable. Suffering is optional."

---

**Debra Rieder** is a Speaker, Best-Selling Author, and Christian Mindset and Wellness Coach who champions mental health for secular and non-secular audiences. Having shared stages with renowned figures like Jack Canfield & James Malinchak, her interactive speeches, workshops, and book are helping put a dent into the Mental Health Crisis for Young Adults and Women.

Best-Seller Book: Overcome Your Inner Critic
Email: Info@DebraRieder.com
Website: DebraRieder.com

# TRAILBLAZER SECRET #15
## Unleash Your Inner Trailblazer:
## 3 Steps to Success
### *Glynis E. Devine*

Trailblazers share a common trait: they know how to leverage their unique strengths to make an impact. In a world where self-doubt often holds people back, here are three transformative steps we can learn from these extraordinary individuals to achieve success:

1. Embrace Your Superpower - Trailblazers understand that just because something comes easily to them doesn't mean it's not valuable. They acknowledge their unique talents and abilities, knowing these set them apart from the crowd. Unfortunately, some people, especially women, find it challenging to do this. We were in Greece on Your Soul Journey, my week-long women's retreat; we did the '7 Reasons Why I Rock' exercise. It made me genuinely sad how long it took a few of these highly successful women leaders to list seven awesome things about themselves! At the leadership conferences I speak at, only a handful of people out of hundreds complete the list within the time I allot - and they're usually men. Trailblazing men and women encourage self-appreciation. Make a list of your strengths and end it with the empowering phrase, "...that's what I'm good at!" This simple exercise can help you acknowledge your worth and build self-confidence.

2. Articulate Your Superpower - Trailblazers understand that their abilities are as unique as a fingerprint; this self-awareness is a powerful predictor of success. Even some successful women in senior leadership roles that I coach struggle with articulating their worth without feeling boastful. Practice listing your strengths out loud, in private at first, and

gradually share them with others. Authentically affirming your superpower opens the door for others to announce theirs, making it a win-win situation for everyone involved.

3. Share Your Impact - Finally, trailblazers excel at evangelizing the impact of their work to the right people. They've learned that everyone is constantly selling, whether it's selling an idea, an opinion, or a perspective.

Apply these three steps to break free from self-doubt and become a powerful contributor to all stakeholders. It's time to unleash your superpower and become the Trailblazer you are meant to be!

---

**Glynis E. Devine** is the President and Chief Empowerment Officer of She-Suite Leaders. As a keynote speaker and solutionist, she works with organizations to take their women leaders to the next level. Sharing her Leadership Catalyst Series in English and French has taken her around the globe. She is a shoe freak and a GiGi to 5 grandchildren.

Instagram: @glynis_e_devine
LinkedIn: @glynisedevinespeaker
Website: shesuiteleaders.com

# TRAILBLAZER SECRET #16
## Embracing Confidence: Overcoming Insecurities and Imposter Syndrome
*Heide Baer*

We all have moments when self-doubt or negative self-talk creeps in. It's natural to feel this way, but what's crucial is how we navigate these emotions. Simply connecting with others can go a long way toward bolstering confidence and generating positivity and momentum. Here is a story to illustrate why I believe this is true.

As a 17-year-old leaving home to embark on a journey of self-discovery through travel and attending university, I was no stranger to insecurities. Like any teenager, my mind was filled with thoughts of what others must think of me. The prospect of meeting new people and forging my path in a world where nobody knew me was both exhilarating and intimidating. But it was precisely during this time that I realized a powerful truth: I had the opportunity to redefine myself in unfamiliar territory.

Embracing this chance, I decided to shed my natural shyness and reserve. I recognized that I needed to take control of how I interacted with others to succeed socially and professionally. I ventured out with newfound knowledge and a desire to present a confident and friendly persona.

The first step in conquering social insecurities at any age is acknowledging that almost everyone, at some point, grapples with similar feelings. The person beside you at that meeting or networking event has likely experienced self-doubt, too. This realization can be remarkably liberating and is a crucial foundation for building confidence.

The next time you find yourself in a professional setting like a meeting or networking event, or even in a casual encounter at the park, I challenge you to take a deep breath, put on a friendly smile, and initiate a conversation with a stranger.

Networking, after all, is about building meaningful connections. By taking the initiative, you enhance your self-esteem and open the door to opportunity. Don't be afraid to ask questions, listen actively, and share your thoughts. I think you'll find that most people are receptive to genuine interactions.

Embracing confidence and initiating conversations can level the playing field. Your voice matters, your ideas are valuable, and you are impactful. I promise.

---

**Heide Baer,** a bookkeeper in BC, Canada, appreciates modern business tools and their ability to empower business owners. She is passionate about helping other small business owners achieve their goals – and about being a good mother, of course!

Facebook: @baeressentialsbooks
LinkedIn: @heideanna
Website: baeressentials.ca/about

# TRAILBLAZER SECRET #17
## Making a Living Laughing
### *Janice Bannister*

"We already have a woman on this month," was the answer from the comedy club booker when I called to get a spot on an open mic night when I started comedy in 2013. I responded, "Okay, I'll call back next month."

A trailblazer needs resilience; as a woman in the stand-up comedy world, the gatekeepers were not supportive 20 years ago. Showing up at clubs week after week, calling and leaving voicemails, and introducing and reintroducing myself to bookers was the way to get stage time. And none of the gigs in the early stage were paid gigs.

Create your Brand as a Trailblazer. Look at what is unique about you and what you must do to make a living off your brand. For me, it was a strong belief in the value of laughter as a mental wellness tool. With my background as a Psychiatric Nurse and my experience working with acute mental patients, I know the science behind the value of laughter. I was quirky and funny and had wonderful stories that worked on stage. The combination of my brand allowed me to get paid gigs and bring workshops to business and conferences. In addition to the brand, you need contracts, bios, and other support information related to your offerings.

Your Art is Your Business, and you are the Product. Selling yourself is never easy, but it is essential. When people ask what I do, I say, "I teach stand-up comedy classes to help you step out of your comfort zone. I'll teach you how to write your authentic stories and share them, which will help you with your public speaking, job collaborations, and relationships in your everyday world". All this in a fun, supportive environment.

Do some business work every day. As an artist, it is easy to work on my Art, writing new jokes, stories, or scripts. But they don't make any money unless I work on the business side of the Art. Every day, I do three things. I work on the art side by writing my own new comedy or workshop material. I work on the business side by calling new or follow-up contacts, pitching shows, and designing new classes/programs. Thirdly, I read something to do with creativity.

Stick with it! Decide if you can do your ART as your job or as a side hustle. I often heard "you can't make a living in the arts" but you can if you are willing to do the work. I loved doing comedy shows, but in my first year, I was paid in beer tickets, bottled water and the occasional basket of chicken wings. Even when I won the Funniest Female competition, I won a Toblerone chocolate bar, an ICBC hat, and 50 bucks. So, I kept a day job to do comedy at night. Then, as I rebranded, I got bolder with my pitches; I started doing workshop for companies on "Laughter as a Wellness Tool". Once my comedy income equalled my day job income, I pivoted to only doing stand-up comedy gigs and workshops. Then, I added classes, private coaching, and now comedy shows for private parties and theatres. Step by step, changing directions when I need to, but always trying something new.

---

**Janice Bannister** is a stand-up comic, storyteller, keynote humourist speaker, TEDx speaker and workshop facilitator. Janice was also a Psychiatric Nurse for fourteen years, so she combines her scientific nerd side with her "flipping the bird" side to entertain her audiences.

She is a two-time winner of BC's Funniest Female competition, and her comedy has been featured on CBC, Women's Network, Just for Laughs, and the Vancouver Fringe Festival.

Janice is the owner and principal instructor of Laughter Zone 101, a stand-up comedy and storytelling school. She designed a Kid's Summer Comedy Camp for Capilano University and teaches classes in Stand-up comedy and Arts for Brain Fitness for the SFU 55+ Continuing Studies Program. Currently, her students range from eight to ninety-two years old.

Janice is a passionate advocate for Mental Wellness and has done inclusive and supportive programming for all persons with mental health challenges.

She was an Entrepreneur of the Year Finalist in the Douglas Collage Self Employment Program (2005), and her business was featured in the Van Sun Business section "The Queen of the Comedy Business." (2014)

She was recently featured in Vancouver Daily Hive as she celebrated her twenty years in stand-up comedy. (2023)

She is also a Mom and the GramaLamaDingDong to three Grandgirls.

Instagram: @laughterzone101
LinkedIn: @janicebannister
Website: laughterzone101.com

> "**MEASURE** YOUR LIFE BY **SATISFACTION!** ~~NOT SUCCESS~~."
>
> ~ Diane Rolston

# TRAILBLAZER SECRET #18
## Your Calling is Calling You Forth
*Jeanine Becker*

After a winding six-year fertility journey to be a solo mama, my daughter Maia - a miracle of love, science and spirit - came into this world. Previously, I had a twenty-year purpose-led career focused on collaborative leadership and systems change. While work was fulfilling, I had an unshakable sense, a deep call, to be a mom. I dreamt of my daughter. In meditation, the sound of her laughter would fill me - even while she was only a prayer.

Following the call to be a mama, even solo, while leading, has been my crazy, impossible dream. I've learned that these visions make our hearts beat faster, pull us to blaze a trail and have us both excited and unsure - these callings are not just pointing us toward what is needed in the world but also our own evolution.

Grounded in 15 years of working with purpose-led leaders and the process of creating my own big dreams, I've identified three polarities, together the **6 C's**, that serve as **Catalysts for Your Calling**. Polarities form a creative tension between two factors that may appear in tension but are interdependent poles. As leaders, we are constantly navigating creative tensions with our strategy - such as being grounded I reality and holding an aspirational vision. Just as you inhale and exhale - choosing between the two poles isn't an option. I go deep into these three polarities with practice and play in my coaching, programs, and book.

To fuel your trailblazing, in this piece, I am offering a taste of these three polarities with simple practices and questions to explore. As you read on, I invite you to bring to mind your deep call, the one that has you feeling excited and unsure. For each polarity - sit with the questions. Notice if one side of the polarity feels easier. Can you sense how each creative tension might be inviting you to stretch? You've got this, *and* for support with your clarity or creation - reach out - your unique call is needed, and it is calling you.

### 6 C's - Catalysts for Your Calling

**Compassion & Curiosity**

**Compassion** – definition: *The potent combination of kindness toward what is hard, a sense of not being alone in the stretch, and presence.*

If your calling seems too big or uncertain, like my desire to be a mama while leading, bring your hand to your heart. Start by taking a breath—honor where you are and what feels challenging. Maybe, like me, you've had a deadline for an important project or the kick-off of a program, your child is sick and wants to snuggle, and there is a pile of dishes in the sink, and you wonder - *is there enough of me to meet this moment?* Notice the tension in your body and breathe compassion into that space. This moment of presence invites our nervous systems to regulate and our awareness to expand. That type of pause allows me to remember that what feels challenging results from receiving what I prayed for.

When I facilitated a cohort of Foundation CEOs, they deeply valued having a space to share, be celebrated, and be seen with compassion - their challenges were familiar struggles. Each leader was stretched - one co-created a new strategy while launching a child into college, another navigated board dynamics and a teething toddler, and each leader drove change while creating an inclusive culture. This first pole is about acknowledging and being with what is hard - with compassion.

From this place of compassion and presence - you are ready to explore the other pole in this first polarity - Curiosity. *The call is a stretch; it's messy and just may be a miracle.*

**Curiosity** - While compassion reminds you that everyone struggles, curiosity invites you to look at what is unique about your mix of desire and challenge. When I taught Negotiation and Collaboration at Stanford, I developed my curriculum to have my students receive key lessons through theory, practice, and reflection - planning for the lessons to be reinforced in their repetition. When I sit with a coaching client, we get curious about how their unique mix of desires, challenges and opportunities is exquisitely designed to call forth their next leadership leap. For example, from this place of deep curiosity, one founder realized that a challenge with a member of his leadership team and an issue with his child invited a new relationship with kind and firm boundaries. Another client recognized that the uncertainty she was sitting with about a promotion reinforced a lesson from her fertility journey - inspired action and surrender. This practice of curiosity invites you to shift from feeling the tension, like you are the rope in a game of tug-of-war, to sensing how all the ropes might be pulling and propelling you forward. This shift in perspective - this miracle - is a sacred shift. To cultivate the conditions for this sacred shift, return to compassion, maybe even gratitude for what feels hard, and get deeply curious. Look for magic.

PRACTICE
Compassion - Invest five minutes to journal:
- Notice and honor what is most challenging about your calling in this moment. Bring awareness to the painful emotions that are present. Be accepting and non-judgemental of what feels hard.
- Write down the ways your challenge is shared by many. For example - every great parent I know has moments of not feeling enough.

- Write down the kind words you long to hear or those you would offer to a dear friend.

Compassion - Bring two minutes of presence:
- Notice where you feel that challenge in your body and what sensations arise.
- Take one slow breath. Then bring a breath of compassion, of kindness, and your exquisite presence to that space. Explore how the sensation just might shift with your mere presence.

Get Curious - Invest five minutes to speak out loud and record yourself:
- If your unique mix of challenges and opportunities is designed to support you, how are you being invited to grow?
- Play the recording and see what sparks for you.

**Capable & Collaborate** - Following your call will require you to honor that you are capable by claiming your unique strengths and require you to acknowledge your limits - and collaborate. One CEO I work with, a mom and CEO of a multi-million-dollar social enterprise, had a vision for how her firm could grow while solo parenting a toddler. In our work together, she claimed her strengths and honoured what she loved to do and her limits. And she created a leadership team she could lean into and hired a director of operations and a chef to cook yummy organic food for her family. By honouring that she is capable *and* collaborating, she was able to limit her work hours, be present for her daughter and commit to her yoga practice while growing her team, revenue, and impact. You are capable and enough. And where can you collaborate for more ease, grace, and impact?

PRACTICE
Capable - Repeat, Reflect and Commit:

- Repeat "I am capable and enough" three times slowly. Invest five minutes journaling about what arose for you as you repeated that phrase.
- Invest another five minutes answering - what is your genius, what is yours to do, and what are your limits?
- Commit to one action based on what you noticed.

Collaborate - Take an Inventory:
- Identify resources, skills, and strengths you could invite for more ease and impact.
- Go beyond what you "need" and allow yourself to consider what would delight you.

**Courage & Care**- The call to blaze a trail often feels crazy, maybe impossible. It will require your courage and your care, but not your confidence. Confidence is the result of taking action - not the prerequisite. Remember the last thing you did that felt edgy; that was a real stretch. How does it seem now? Our edge expands with our action. Your courage will propel your impact. For this call to beckon you - there is something edgy in it. That bubbling sense of aliveness - is the marker for a threshold (or a few) you will need to cross-thresholds that will test and grow you. At the same time - this calling isn't a sprint you can hustle through. Maybe, like many of my clients, as someone committed and responsible, you've tried pushing harder, taking more on yourself - struggling under the weight of that effort and without results that meet your vision. One client stepped into coaching as her promotion to the C Suite was imminent - fully capable, deeply anxious and challenged by her need to learn enough to "get it right." That effort, the hustle, is depleting and often fueled by a sense that we and our impact are not enough. Care, on the other hand, is the clean and renewable fuel of desire and heart. It honours where you are and who you are. It follows a spark of inspiration and invites you to live into the sentence - "it would be even better if ___." In working with that client, we held her and her big vision with care - and consistently discovered the next tiny and courageous step. By the time she was sitting in her corner office, when I asked how it felt, she answered, "This is where I belong".

Can you sense why your calling is alive for you - the threshold it asks you to cross? To cross that threshold - bring your courage and allow yourself to be fueled by your care - for yourself and your impact. Choose both.

PRACTICE
Courage - Invest five minutes exploring:
- What is the next tiny and courageous step for you to take? Notice if there is a step you can see but don't want to take - because it is too big or too little.
- What would need to be true about this next step for it to qualify as "courageous" for you?

Care - Find a place that feels good to you, where you feel a sense of warmth and lightness -, the bathtub, your meditation cushion, a walk in the trees, sitting in the sunshine, or while snuggling your little one. From that place, sit with these questions:
- What is the next step that moves your calling forward that feels light or that has a spark of aliveness for you?
- If you could have it any way - how would the next step unfold?

**Your Invitation**
Global warming is in our weather reports; gender equity is on a backward slide, and our systems are shaking and new, hopefully, more equitable and liberating ones are being conceived. In Chinese, the word for crisis combines the characters of danger and opportunity (or change point). In the context of this crisis, I trust your calling is needed and that your impact is part of weaving new living systems. I spent a decade as a professor of collaboration. I coach and consult and am passionate about that place where personal growth meets

strategy and collaborative approaches to impact. I dedicate this piece to my daughter and my mom, my bedrock of support, because "solo" parenting Maia while leading has been my master class in delight, surrender, leaning into support, and being on purpose together. Like my journey and that of my clients, I invite you to blaze your trail fueled by the **6 C's** - your compassion and curiosity, acknowledging you are capable and need to collaborate, and taking action with courage and care. Your calling is needed, and it is calling you forth.

---

**Jeanine Becker** is a coach, facilitator, speaker, and systems strategist. She is passionate about how we are on purpose together, and she partners with purpose-led leaders and multi-sector collaborations to scale their impact sustainably through generative relationships, thriving cultures, and emergent strategies. Her clients are leaders in foundations, corporations, non-profits and networks who are moved by the crises of our times, sense the systems at play, and see possibility.

Jeanine's Individual and team clients have included leaders at Philanthropies Northwest, World Education Services, the Amgen Foundation, the World Bank, Slack, ParadigmIQ, MedZed, BART, the Central Park Conservancy, SiteLab Urban Studios, and Uncommon Cacao. Through her business, Co-Lab Leadership Group, and as a member of the Impact Networks Collaborative, Jeanine's Impact Network and multi-sector collaboration clients have included World Pulse, the Center for Dialogue and Resolution, Conveners.org. the Impact, and the Collaborative for Frontier Finance. She also edited a supplement in the Stanford Social Innovation Review focused on cross-sector leadership and authored multiple pieces including "The Need for Cross Sector Collaboration" and the "Essentials of Cross Sector Leadership."

Jeanine's work is influenced by over a decade of teaching Negotiation and Collaboration at Stanford, closing thousands of deals on four continents, as well as ancient wisdom and current research in neuroscience and systems theory

In addition to writing her book on the 6 C's and articles on impact networks, collaborative leadership and driving impact, inclusively, she loves sharing insights, stories, practices, and research about the 6 C's for Catalyzing Your Calling in her Online Group called Purpose-led Mamas. She believes that being a mama in these times calls many of us to not only care deeply about our own children, but also to create sustainable systems for their future. She explores the synergy between our most present parenting lessons and our next leadership leap. She is so passionate about her Purpose-Led Mama program because her clients are creating results for their impact and lives that exceed their big dreams by embracing the 6 Cs and allowing their unique deep calls to call them.

"Jeanine's natural and genuine way of being is infectious with an audience. Participants at our various events reflected that the exercises Jeanine led helped them share with more authenticity and vulnerability. I was so pleased to see our community connecting from these places and sharing the impact it had on them. Whether at Wisdom Women events, Wisdom 2.0 Business or on the main stage in front of 2000 at Wisdom 2.0, I'm grateful for Jeanine's grounded and professional presence and that she's able to bring that to our events with so much heart and insight." - Michelle Stransky

FB Group: http://bit.ly/FBGroup-PurposeLedMamas
LinkedIn: @beckerjeanine
Linktree: linktr.ee/jeaninebecker

# TRAILBLAZER SECRET #19
## The AI Trailblazer:
## Where Tech Meets Awesomeness
### *Jo-Ann Wolloff*

Do you fancy yourselves as trailblazers? On my journey to become a Certified Artificial Intelligence (AI) Consultant, I realized that being a trailblazer in AI isn't about wearing a fancy explorer's hat. Still, it does involve a healthy dose of curiosity and courage to navigate the tech wilderness.

Okay, let's talk about innovation. It's similar to when you realize putting pineapple on pizza is a game-changer. Trailblazers in AI embrace innovation like we're on a quest to find the ultimate pizza topping. We're dreamers envisioning a future where AI doesn't just predict your pizza preferences but also makes the perfect pie.

Let's talk diversity—it's about having a menu with something for everyone. Trailblazing in AI means we appreciate diverse perspectives and backgrounds. It's like having a pizza party with various flavours because why limit ourselves to just one?

In AI, we push boundaries, lead in research, and redefine what's possible. We're not afraid to toss new ingredients into the tech mix. We don't believe in limits.

We are AI mentors—guiding the next generation like culinary instructors teaching the art of pizza-making. We're all about helping young talents discover their flavour in the world of AI. And, just like any good pizza chef, we advocate for equal access to opportunities in AI for everyone. We have training and memberships to get started without reinventing the wheel. We even train you to become Mentors yourself. I tell my students that trailblazing in AI is about stirring things up, like tossing pizza dough in the air. It's about showing that anyone can make their mark in the tech world, regardless of where they come from. As a trailblazer, we're the pizza chef creating something incredible for everyone to savour.

Being a trailblazer in AI is like being the chef at the most incredible pizza joint in town. We're mixing innovation, diversity, and a dash of mentorship to create a tech masterpiece. My story and yours aren't just chapters but recipes for success in the AI kitchen. So, keep trailblazing because the world of AI needs more of our unique flavours!

---

**Jo-Ann Wolloff** AI Certified Consultant/Mentor and an Affiliate Marketing/Mentor. I specialize in slowly bringing entrepreneurs into the ever-changing world of artificial intelligence (AI) with tons of energy and fun.

LinkedIn: @joann-wolloff
Linktree: linktr.ee/joannwolloff
Website: myaffiliateangel.com

# TRAILBLAZER SECRET #20
## It's Not What We Build, But How We Build…And for Who?
### *Jodi Huettner*

I am an engineer-turned-entrepreneur and a trailblazer for gender-inclusive systems change. Here's why.

We are facing a daunting skilled labour shortfall over the next decade in Canada, and because our construction growth projections continue to increase, we need women to help fill the gap. However, women remain under-represented in construction trades and active STEMM jobs, not because of a lack of ability or desire.

Picture this: I started my career as an engineer in training over ten years ago, supervising environmental remediation projects in remote locations along the coast of beautiful British Columbia. I struggled to do my job wearing the required personal protective equipment (PPE) because it was made to fit the average man. My so-called protective equipment didn't sit where it should on my body, put me at increased risk of injury, made it difficult to take hygiene breaks, and denied me the same freedom to work that my male counterparts enjoyed.

I felt unprofessional, uncomfortable, unsafe, and utterly…othered. That inspired me to start a business (Helga Wear), applying engineering design principles to making safety apparel for women's bodies and advocating for inclusive policy and enforcement standards.

What keeps me trailblazing to this day are stories like Joan's: Her mother called me looking for women's safety coveralls because Joan had been showing up for family dinners with burns on her wrist, neck, and chest. Joan is a young apprentice welder. She says there's nothing she can do about it; she just doesn't fit into the welding gloves and safety coveralls provided at work. Joan loves welding, is good at it, and doesn't want to jeopardize getting hired after her apprenticeship by complaining about her PPE. Joan is not alone - feeling incapable of advocating for herself.

I trailblaze for all the women like Joan because I am uniquely positioned to advocate. I wear the iron ring of an engineer. Although the practice of designing PPE using women's body dimensions and gender-based standards is NOT rocket science, I continue to face resistance to its adoption in the industry. Being a trailblazer means being the first to do something challenging, incredibly rewarding, and, in many cases, before it becomes profitable.

In addition to running Helga Wear, I now consult employers in industries where women and minorities are under-utilized, helping them take measurable and meaningful steps (like proper-fitting PPE) that engage and incorporate a multitude of voices - evolving their systems to include diverse experiences right from design.

---

**Jodi Huettner** has a degree in mechanical engineering with a concentration in computer-integrated manufacturing and a law minor, and she now uses that knowledge to inform her safety clothing design practice and advocacy work.

Facebook: @HelgaWearInc
LinkedIn: @jodi-huettner
Website: helgawear.com

# TRAILBLAZER SECRET #21
## Trailblazing a Path for Filipinos with IgA Vasculitis
*Karissa Ramos*

Have you ever heard of a rare disease called IgA Vasculitis? I didn't, either, until my boyfriend was diagnosed with it at the height of the pandemic.

The pandemic made it difficult to find information and support for his condition, especially in the Filipino context. That's why, after almost a year of contemplating, I started a support group for Filipinos with IgA Vasculitis in 2021.

I know running a support group is a serious obligation, but I'm committed to helping others facing the same challenges as my boyfriend and me.

Now, two years later, our community has more than 550 members. We've also partnered with the Vasculitis Special Interest Group (Vasculitis SIG) of the Philippine Rheumatology Association (PRA) to produce videos answering the frequently asked questions about IgA Vasculitis. In a meeting with them, we discussed our future goals and plans for the community.

We've also launched a Facebook page called "Henoch-Schönlein Purpura - IgA Vasculitis Filipino Support" to reach more people. The page now has more than 300 followers.

Occasionally, we receive messages from group members thanking us for creating the group. One member wrote, "I'm so grateful for this support group. It's been a lifesaver for me. I don't know what I would do without it." Messages like this fill our hearts and make us continue.

But seeing how our members support each other through their experiences and stories is a testament that we are all trailblazers in this story. I just lit the fire, but the whole community keeps it blazing.

My boyfriend and I are committed to helping more Filipinos with IgA Vasculitis in any way we can. We hope our support group can continue to grow and provide a safe and supportive space for people facing this challenging disease.

---

**Karissa Ramos** is a virtual assistant from the Philippines, "Tita Ganda" to her seven nieces and nephews, baby princess to her boyfriend, and founder of Henoch-Schönlein Purpura – IgA Vasculitis Filipino Support Community.

Email: karissaworks@gmail.com
Facebook Group: @hspsupportph
LinkedIn: @karissa-paula-ramos

# TRAILBLAZER SECRET #22
## Charting Your Course: Elevate Your Life Through Gratitude, Appreciation and Kindness
### *Kathy Fester*

Life presents a complex tapestry of triumphs and trials. Weaved within this design are pathways to success, unveiled through expressions of gratitude, appreciation, and attentive intuition.

Gratitude is a guiding star amid life's bewildering maze. It brightens our perspective, transforming obstacles into learning opportunities. Reflecting daily on our blessings sharpens our focus on the positive, enabling us to summon resilience during challenging phases.

Appreciation, akin to gratitude, helps build a step-by-step ladder toward success. Acknowledging our small victories creates confidence, propelling us towards our larger goals. It's an ode to progress, subtly whispering, "You're on the right track."

In the midst of our loud world, intuition serves as a quietly persistent compass, nudging us towards decisions that align with our inner values. Living by our promptings adds a unique vibrancy to our life journey, steering us toward authenticity. That 'gut feeling' is more than mere instinct; it's our soul's way of ensuring we stay true to our inner essence even amid tumultuous times.

This wholesome harmony of gratitude, appreciation, and intuition cultivates a fertile field for joy and happiness to grow.

Even when storms strike, they nourish our roots, making us stronger and more adaptable.

Remember, life's not a sprint; it's a unique marathon designed just for you. Embrace your pace, cherish the teachable moments, and heed your intuition's whispers. This loving combination will pave your trail to a life of fulfillment, allowing you to blaze through life's challenges confidently. Let gratitude light your path, let appreciation fuel your journey, and let your intuition be your compass.

Embark on this journey filled with gratitude, appreciation, and intuition. You'll soon realize that trailblazing through life's challenges isn't just about the destination; it's about who you become along the way.

---

**Kathy Fester** is an expert business relationship marketing strategist, author, entrepreneur, master teacher & life-long learner. She assists individuals in navigating life through the practice of gratitude & exemplifies her teachings by maintaining a cheerful demeanour and living by her advice. She aids businesses in harnessing the potential of relationship marketing by guiding them to establish genuine human connections through gratitude. Kathy promotes gratitude and helps people navigate life through its practice. Her dedication to the subject is evident through her position as a co-founder of the Gratitude and Appreciation Summit.

Kathy possesses love, passion, care and, above all, kindness. She is an expert in the field of relationship marketing. Kathy actively demonstrates Gratitude in her own life by practicing what she preaches and maintaining a cheerful demeanour; she embodies the principles she teaches, making her an authentic and trustworthy source of guidance.

Kathy has over 30 years of experience as a master teacher, teaching students from Kindergarten to Grade 12. Her multifaceted expertise, genuine approach, and dedication to gratitude and relationship marketing make her a highly respected figure in her field. Her teachings and presentations have positively impacted numerous individuals and businesses, while her love for learning and creativity further enhance her well-rounded personality. Her life's mantra is to live through Kindness, Gratitude and Appreciation and Promptings!

LinkedIn: @kathyfester
Linktree: linktr.ee/kathyfester
Website: promptings.com/?sponsor=kathyfester

> "THERE WILL BE PEOPLE **WHO CHANGE YOU** & **<u>PEOPLE YOU CHANGE</u>**. *IMPACT WISELY.*"
>
> ~ Diane Rolston

# TRAILBLAZER SECRET #23
## Called by God to Blaze a Trail
### Kendra Dahlstrom

Blazing a trail prompted by God is a profound and spiritually charged endeavour. It is a calling that transcends the ordinary as you embark on a path that is divinely ordained. In many religious and spiritual traditions, following God's guidance to carve out a unique path holds great significance.

It does not matter if you think you are ready. It does not matter if you believe you are worthy. It does not matter if what you are told makes sense. It does not matter if you know "how" it will unfold. You may feel like the least qualified person to be blazing the trail you are called to. The trail will be rooted in your trauma, healing, and wounds because you can most powerfully help those with whom you empathize and relate along the path. In the following pages, I share my story and how it prepared me to answer a calling from God to blaze a trail in the health and wellness space.

*"The only way out is through."*
*- Robert Frost*

The weight of a lifetime of struggles, abuse, and trauma had taken its toll, and I had yet to acknowledge and confront it all honestly. I was trapped in a state of resistance, judging myself and seeking solace in my accomplishments. Though I had a loving family, I couldn't find true joy within myself.

One morning, tears streamed down my face as I cried out, desperate for answers. "Jesus, what is my purpose? Please help me!" He promptly answered, "You are here to show people my love and light in a new way. You will bring people together and bridge the divide."

I felt inadequate and unqualified. I didn't know what this meant or how any of this would happen. That day, I embarked unexpectedly on a profound journey of self-discovery, truth-seeking, healing, and empowerment. I was now sure that God had a greater purpose for me, a calling that I had yet to fulfill.

*Divine Calling:* When God prompts you to blaze a trail, it often begins with a deep, unmistakable inner calling. This calling may come in the form of a profound realization, a vision, an audible voice, or a feeling that you are meant for something greater. It is a moment of spiritual awakening that cannot be ignored.

*Guidance and Inspiration:* When you receive this divine prompting, you will experience the ebb and flow of inspiration and guidance. You will feel a sense of purpose and clarity about the direction you should take. It's as if God has laid a roadmap for you, illuminating the steps they need to follow.

*Overcoming Obstacles:* Blazing a trail, primarily when guided by God, is not without its challenges. You may face obstacles, doubts, and resistance from others. However, your unwavering faith and trust in God's plan will sustain you through these difficult times.

*Faith and Surrender:* Following God's prompting requires deep faith and surrender to a higher purpose. It involves relinquishing your plans and desires in favour of God's plan. This surrender can be liberating and challenging, necessitating letting go of control.

*Impact and Transformation*: The trails blazed under divine guidance are not just personal journeys; they have the potential to transform the lives of others. You become a beacon of hope, leading the way for others seeking their path. Your actions and choices inspire those around you.

*Spiritual Growth:* Blazing a trail prompted by God is a profound avenue for spiritual growth. It tests your faith, resilience, and commitment to the divine path. Along the way, you will experience personal transformation and a deepening of your relationship with God.

*Legacy and Heritage:* When you follow God's prompting, you leave behind a legacy and heritage that endures for generations. Your actions and teachings become foundational to your communities, leaving a lasting impact on the world.

*A Source of Hope:* In a world filled with uncertainty and challenges, blazing a trail under God's guidance is a source of hope. You remind us that we are not alone in our journey and that there is a higher purpose to our lives.

When prompted by God to blaze a trail, you are embarking on a sacred journey that is both challenging and rewarding. It is a path of faith, surrender, and profound spiritual growth. You, in essence, become a conduit for God's will, leaving behind a legacy that continues to inspire and guide future generations.

**Kendra Dahlstrom** specializes in transforming people from the inside out. Kendra is a Coach and Speaker committed to healing millions in her lifetime. Her health and wellness app, Soul Star Awakening, provides the purpose-driven with on-demand access to healing treatments and meditations to experience more harmony, joy, love,  and God-inspired flow in their lives. Kendra is a survivor of severe trauma and abuse, which inspires her mission to provide a healing space and community inspired by Jesus' love for us that brings more inner peace, self-love, mindfulness, and clarity.

*"May my meditation be pleasing to Him, for I rejoice in the Lord."*
*– Psalm 143:5*

Email: team@kendradahlstrom.com
Facebook: @spirituality_and_leadership
Website : kendradahlstrom.com

# TRAILBLAZER SECRET #24
## Reclaiming My Power
### *Kimberly Lyall*

"Why don't you wear your Canada jacket to the awards ceremony?"

My husband's question brought an immediate rush of anxiety. "Maybe" I replied, as I added the jacket to my suitcase. I knew it was a good idea, but my heart hurt at the thought. I would decide what to wear the morning of the event.

I first got the jacket as an 18-year-old youth exchange student living in England. Red and white with maple leaves, it looked like a Canadian flag. Wearing the jacket became an honour as complete strangers shared with me their love and respect for my country.

In my 20's, I wore the jacket as I led Canada Day events in my community and province.

I also wore it as a motivational speaker throughout North America.

At age 26, I was part of the Canadian delegation to the World YWCA Conference in Australia, where we confronted global issues facing women. We wore the Canada jackets with pride.

I returned home from that trip to become the CEO of the oldest regional tourism organization in western Canada. I made the jacket our uniform and wore it for ten more years, representing southern Alberta to the world.

Then, at the height of my career, I was fired without cause.

I'd reported harassment by a board member to my Board Chair, a woman I considered a mentor and friend. The police advised that my harasser should be removed from the organization. Instead, I was removed.

So were the jackets, and I hadn't worn mine since.

A few days after asking the question, my husband and I were in Ottawa. I was there to accept an award from the Queen's representative, the Governor General of Canada, for an innovative community oral history project I'd created following my firing.

On the morning of that very formal event, I didn't allow myself to think about it. I just put on the jacket. To say I stood out amongst the other recipients in their black formal wear is an understatement!

When my name was called, and I walked forward to receive the award, the Governor General had a massive smile on his face. "I LOVE your jacket!" he delightedly told me. I couldn't believe my ears!

I gave my acceptance speech and had just returned to my seat when suddenly the Governor General halted the ceremony to exclaim to the room "I just LOVE Kimberly's jacket!" I sat even taller.

When the ceremony ended, we were to rise and sing the national anthem. Suddenly, the Governor General announced, "I would like Kimberly to come forward and lead us in the singing of O Canada!" My heart pounded as I walked to stand by our flag. It was the most surreal and amazing experience to lead the singing of our national anthem in front of the Governor General of Canada, and my fellow award winners and guests from across the country!

The surprises didn't end there. Following the ceremony, everyone crowded into a ballroom for pictures with the Governor General. However, my husband and I were whisked to another room, where we were given a private audience with him! He was especially thrilled when my husband removed his flag jacket and handed it to the Governor General to wear for a photo.

All my life I have worked to inspire change and empower others. But when I was fired, I was hurt and humiliated, and my confidence was destroyed.

Being reminded of my strength and exceptionality in such an amazing way renewed my connection to hope and courage when I needed it most. Not only was I in the thick of legal action against my termination at the time of the ceremony, but three weeks later, my husband underwent rare surgery to save his life.

It would have been so easy to wear a black dress to the ceremony and blend into the crowd. Putting on the jacket – a symbol of who I had been before being fired - was hard. But I did it to take my power back and to reclaim an essential part of myself. I had no idea the incredible experience I would have because I wore it!

Every day we have choices. Trailblazers choose to face their fears and do what they know is right. Yes, I was fired. But because I found the courage to reclaim my power by wearing the jacket, the Governor General of Canada picked me out of the crowd and celebrated me. I was reminded of who I really am.

Now, whenever I am tempted let fear get in the way of my dreams, I remember that day and am inspired to keep blazing trails!

**Kimberly Lyall** is a multi-award-winning speaker who 'Lights up Leaders', helping change-makers create impact. Audiences say she leaves them feeling full of light, hope, and confidence that they can overcome any obstacle!

Kimberly has created success for organizations, governments, and communities throughout North America as a transformational leadership specialist. Alongside her many accomplishments, Kimberly's experiences rebuilding an organization following employee fraud and death, as well as grieving the death of her own husband, make her uniquely equipped to support leaders navigating major change.

*"People are still talking about your presentation a week later, and those that missed it are looking for the recording. Your message certainly struck a chord with many!"*

- Marnie Hamp,
Sr. Marketing Manager
FujiFilm Sonosite

*"When you are on stage you shine so bright! We see the light in you and that allows us to see the light in ourselves. All the notes and insights that I shared with my team after the conference came from your presentation."*

- Karissa Schlaht,
Director Women in Business,
Alberta Treasury Branch

Facebook: @kimberlylyall
LinkedIn: @KimberlyLyall
Website: kimberlylyall.com

# TRAILBLAZER SECRET #25
## Trailblazing My Path
### *Kristine Daruca*

It took me eight years to discover my identity as a Trailblazer and truly understand its meaning. I had no idea how strong, confident, and capable I could be as a woman or that I was who I am now.

My early life was marked by poverty and a broken family. My mother left when I was 19, and shortly after, my father passed away. Amid this chaos, I felt utterly lost.

At 19, I began living with a partner, hoping to escape reality, but I was gravely mistaken. Instead, I found myself trapped in an abusive relationship. Even during my pregnancy, my ex-partner would physically assault me, slapping my face, pulling my hair, and throwing objects at me until I bled from the assault— an almost daily occurrence. I can still feel the trauma the blows inflicted, the pain from wounds, and I hold remorse for staying. I endured all the pain because, in my mind, I didn't want a broken family. I suffered from everything for two years until I finally left to escape the abuse. It wasn't that easy, but I did.

I asked God's guidance, prayed and asked him to give me a sign and lead me the way.

Eight years later, I stand here, living the best years of my life. I've endured a lot of pain, but that didn't stop me from trailblazing a new path away from the abuse. I am now blessed to be living happily with my wonderful, supportive partner, who has treated me like a queen - something I never experienced in the past. Together, we are thriving as we raise our four beautiful children, and I always give them the absolute best in life and shower them with the unconditional love I never received but so desperately craved as a child.

My journey proves that no matter what you've been through, where you've come from, or the obstacles that stand in your way, you can rewrite your story and build the life you want. All you need is the will to keep going and the faith that your circumstances don't define you. If I can do it, anyone can.

You can find your inner strength even when you feel completely lost and broken. If you keep pushing forward, stay true to yourself, and never give up, things can get better, and you can start to heal and trailblaze your path.

---

**Kristine Daruca** is an experienced and dedicated Virtual Assistant with over three years of experience in freelancing and a mum of 4 kids.

Instagram: @itsmedarucakristine
LinkedIn: @KristineDaruca

# TRAILBLAZER SECRET #26
## Money Isn't Evil – Charge What You're Worth
### *Leah Grant*

When I answered the call to be a spiritual teacher, mentor and guide, I expected some trials to build the character and strength necessary to fulfill my purpose. I never considered my approach would be the opposite of the deeply ingrained mindset of poverty consciousness held as a badge of honor by many in the spiritual industry.

From running a marketing consulting firm serving tech companies and then coaching million-dollar-plus financial services advisors and executives at companies like Google, Microsoft and Disney, it didn't occur to me to NOT charge what I'm worth. However, as soon as I revealed the investment to hire me spiritually, I received some shocking feedback:

It started with virtue signaling. Fellow spiritual teachers wondered if I knew they gave away their best stuff for free. Then, it continued with shaming. Some prospective clients said, "If you cared about people, you would charge much less."

When neither of those tactics succeeded, a few attempted to discredit me, stating that I must be a charlatan because a genuinely spiritual person wouldn't ask for so much money.

Willing to be wrong, I checked in with God, who assured me to stay the course. This validation was refreshing as something profound inside me always felt that it's not money that is evil; it's the way money is worshipped that can be.

Money is energy. Humanity would benefit from those aligned with God having cash to commit to movements. Why many believe the spiritual industry should rebuke wealth and serve without fair exchange baffles me.

Most small business owners go into business to serve a need and make money. However, running a spiritual business and supporting yourself beyond barely surviving became taboo, and charging your worth became synonymous with not caring.

I'm busting that myth and calling forth spiritual stewards of wealth to slay poverty consciousness and teach thriving over surviving, happiness over suffering, and success over struggling. Sometimes, being a trailblazer means doing something evident in other industries but not in yours.

---

**Leah Grant** is a multi-published International best-selling author, podcaster (Adventures in Mysticism), creator of Timeline Transformation™, Ecstatic Meditation™, Frequency Elevation™, and Journaling Inspiration. She is a speaker, Master Certified Coach, Certified NLP Practitioner, Master Certified Intuitive, and Star Magic Healer.

Facebook, Instagram and YouTube: @leahthemystic
Website: MysticalSWAG.com

# TRAILBLAZER SECRET #27
## Making the World Accessible. The Business Benefits of Accessibility
*Linda Hunt*

In an increasingly interconnected and diverse world, businesses that embrace accessibility contribute to a more inclusive society and unlock many benefits for their own success. From expanding customer reach to fostering a positive brand image, the advantages are substantial and will help the business to blaze a trail.

1. **Expanded Market Reach:** By making your business accessible, you tap into a significant market share—22% of the population has some form of disability.
2. **Enhanced Customer Loyalty:** Prioritizing accessibility fosters customer loyalty. People appreciate businesses that consider diverse needs.
3. **Improved Reputation and Brand Image:** Accessibility initiatives promote a positive brand image.
4. **Inclusive Hiring and Employee Satisfaction:** Embracing accessibility opens the door to a vast talent pool.
5. **Legal Compliance and Risk Mitigation:** Compliance with accessibility regulations is a legal requirement and a strategic move. Non-compliance can lead to fines and legal complications, negatively impacting the bottom line.
6. **Innovation and Market Leadership:** Businesses that proactively integrate accessibility into their products, services, and spaces often find themselves at the forefront of innovation.
7. **Positive Public Relations:** Accessibility initiatives generate positive public relations.
8. **Adaptability to Demographic Changes:** With an aging population, the percentage of people with disabilities is expected to rise.

In conclusion, the benefits of making businesses accessible extend far beyond compliance. They touch every aspect of business operations. Embracing accessibility is not just a social responsibility; it's a strategic move that unlocks a world of opportunities.

---

**Linda Hunt** is an Award-Winning Accessibility Consultant, Speaker, Podcaster and Author. CEO of Accessibility Solutions, an accessibility consulting firm that aids businesses and organizations in remedying barriers for people with disabilities. Their mission is Making the World Accessible. Linda is the Treasurer of Citizens with Disabilities – Ontario—and a member of The Rick Hansen Foundation – Accessibility Professional Network. Linda is a Certified Community Champion on the United Nations Convention on the Rights of Persons with Disabilities and its Optional Protocol. Linda was elected to Brantford City Council in 2022. She is the first person with a physical disability elected as a Brantford City Councillor.

Linda first became a person with a disability in 2004. Since then, she has become a dedicated advocate for all things related to accessibility. Based in Brantford, ON, Linda and her husband Greg have been married for 35 years and are the proud parents of 2 adult children.

Email: linda@solutions4accessibility.com
LinkedIn: @lindahuntaccessibility
Website: solutions4accessibility.com

# TRAILBLAZER SECRET #28
## The Story of the Lavender Farm
### *Lorraine Peters*

I believe that to be fully in tune with your body is to learn from our natural world. To source out what is healthy and naturally provided by the earth. To find products that are not harmful to the environment, ourselves, or our families. It is not easy or convenient to source natural products. Still, I have learned firsthand how essential it is to take the time, and I believe that with some guidance, everyone can learn to feel good on the inside and the outside by using natural products.

My trail-blazing journey took an exciting turn when I had the chance to work on a Lavender farm. I have visited the lavender farm twice; both were for ten days. Walking through the fields, immersed in the smell of lavender, is a unique sensory experience. Working at the farm means I have been involved from the beginning, the planting to the end, the harvest and the bottling of the lavender oil. I have learned so much that as I cook with and diffuse the lavender, I appreciate knowing where the product comes from and how much lavender is necessary to create a single ounce. I have been able to cook with it confidently. The best is diffusing the lavender throughout my home, car, or trailer; it is a calming oil for everyone.

My experience at the lavender farm encouraged me to go to another farm in Fort St. John, BC, a black spruce farm. We were there for a week, where we could harvest in the winter, putting the boughs in the vats. Being involved in the production of black spruce oil solidified for me how vital black spruce is for both physical health and is a soothing meditative oil for mental health. Its powerful and soothing scent reinforces its ancient gifts. Pushing the black spruce down, we watched as the oil came out; I then realized that our earth provides what we need to thrive.

My trail-blazing journey is a quiet and serene reconnection with the earth, and I share my experiences to inspire others to know our natural world on their own.

---

**Lorraine Peters** has always been interested in helping people learn to be in tune with their bodies and use what nature provides. She offers education on self-care and living a chemical-free lifestyle. She lives in Brantford, Ontario; she is an entrepreneur, wife, mother, grandmother, and great-grandmother. Lorraine is a lifelong learner with diverse skills, from reflexologist to florist, all focused on helping people live at their best, feel healthy, and celebrate life.

Email: lgpeters07@hotmail.com
Website: lorrainepeters.shesgotleggz.ca

# TRAILBLAZER SECRET #29
## Secret Keys to Life and More
### *Marina Leung*

Life is like a series of waves. Some waves are fun to ride; others are wipeouts. Nevertheless, there are essential keys that empower us to ride the huge waves, regardless of difficulty or outcome.

- Be authentic, respectful, humble, and courteous.
- Find one thing you enjoy and focus on the passion for doing such an activity.
- Surround yourself with smarter people than you versus people who tell you what you want to hear.
- Have mentors you admire who are successful and actively practice what they teach.
- Have a morning routine which includes time for affirmations and exercise.
- Calendar all personal and work events. If it's not recorded there, it doesn't exist.
- Give, whether it'd be time, money, or both, with no expectations of receiving anything in return.
- Spend time with people who positively influence your life, and limit time with those who take away valuable time and energy.
- Measure only against yourself and not others.
- Trust but continually verify.
- Invest in personal development.
- Delegate things that are below your pay grade.
- Be in the present moment as we live only between each breath we take.

**Marina Leung** is a professional real estate consultant, real estate investor, mentor, speaker, author, and philanthropist. When it comes to real estate, her skillset is unparalleled to those of her peers, especially when it comes to negotiation and collaboration. Her attention to detail is like no other, and she treats her client's money like it is hers.  Marina's approach to business and life is unique in many ways because she thinks and operates outside the box, as no two people are the same, and no two transactions are the same. Marina is passionate about real estate and loves speaking about personal development and life's secrets to happiness.

Instagram: @marinaleungrealestate
Website: MarinaLeung.com

# TRAILBLAZER SECRET #30
## Blazing Your Trail:
## From Expectations to Expertise
### *Rai Hyde Cornell*

Sometimes, you need to hit a dead end in your life to find your true path.

Mine came in 2014 while working as a Triage Specialist, sitting in a Texas mental hospital across from a man coming down from methamphetamine as I waited to do his intake form for the third time. How did I end up here?

I was raised by two police officers who were dysfunctional parents with traditional expectations. To fill those expectations, I earned three degrees in psychology and human behavior before (painfully) realizing I was on a very wrong path.

So, I changed course and blazed a new trail for myself. You likely know the feeling.

Now, in 2023, not only do I run a successful full-service content marketing agency with a stellar reputation for quality content, copy, and creative marketing. I'm also known as the leading expert in psychology-infused marketing.

Here's how you can become a trailblazer, too:

1. *Mindset Shift: Be Unapologetic.* Own your story by deciding Mindset Shift: Be Unapologetic. Own your story by deciding that you're done being afraid of people finding out, you're done with feeling ashamed, and you're done apologizing for the decisions you've made in the past that led you here.

2. *Perspective Shift: Be Unbiased & Curious.* If someone came across your timeline, what would they see? What would intrigue them? What would catch their eye? What in your history makes people lean in closer?

3. *Shift: Be Passionate.* Sometimes, we realize our daily lives are devoid of the thing we were once passionate about. Take time to get back to what truly lights you up and energizes you.

4. *Role Shift: Be a Teacher.* We're taught to make our livings by being doers. But your most powerful impact can come from being a teacher a thought leader. The more you speak up, the more minds you'll open and the more change you'll effect.

Being a trailblazer isn't just about forging a path that others can follow. It's about forging a path that you can be proud of. What will you be proud to leave behind? What trail will you blaze?

---

**Rai Hyde Cornell** is the CEO and Marketing Strategist at Cornell Content Marketing. With 16+ years in online marketing and writing, Rai has worked with hundreds of businesses, helping them grow and achieve their goals organically with psychology-informed strategies, messaging, and branding.

Book a Call: calendly.com/rairose
LinkedIn: @CornellContentMarketing
Website: cornellcontentmarketing.com

# TRAILBLAZER SECRET #31
## How to Go from Baggage and Burnout to Blazing Your Brilliance
### Robyn Queen

*"Your journey is your wealth. Each of us carries a spark. Some let it flicker, while others let it blaze." - Robyn Queen*

At the tender age of six, my world was rocked by a catastrophic car accident that left me with a severe brain injury. Doctors issued grim predictions, suggesting I wouldn't survive. But I defied those odds. My mother, steadfast in her faith, looked past this prognosis and named me her 'Miracle Child.' She saw a future for me when others could not, advocating tirelessly.

I found myself one of the few students of color in my school while grappling with unique learning challenges; I was met with biases. "She's a sweet little black girl, but she won't go far," they conjectured, unable to see beyond my struggles. Yet, one brilliant educator dared to look beyond these limitations, recognizing my potential and fanning the spark within me. Her act of faith and fortitude charted a new course for my life.

Years later, I worked within the confines of a system that once underestimated me. I labored tirelessly, often sacrificing my needs, trying to fit into a mold not designed for me. The consequence? It was a ferocious battle with burnout—an all-consuming state of emotional, physical, and mental exhaustion that threatened to snuff out my brilliance.

That burnout was my wake-up call. It was time for radical change. I aligned myself with God's will and purpose for my life, stepping away from the traditional school system to reclaim my narrative and venture into uncharted territory. This new path allowed me to leverage my unique understanding and experiences to make a lasting impact.

Despite your challenges or struggles, you have what it takes to rise above, live your dream life, and make a significant impact. My friend, will you let the blaze of your unique light shine? The world is keenly waiting.

---

**Robyn Queen,** affectionately known as the 'Queen Educator' and Brilliance Coach, carries a rich 20-year education, leadership, and advocacy legacy. As the founder of Everybody Educate LLC, she comes highly recommended for her commitment to unlocking potential and inspiring excellence. A transformative speaker and coach, Queen's proven methods have positively shifted the lives of countless individuals. Through her Brilliance Coaching Program, she equips others to harness their unique strengths, fostering sustainable success within and beyond the classroom.

LinkedIn: @RobynQueenEducator
Website: robynqueen.com/contact
Website: everybodyeducate.com

# TRAILBLAZER SECRET #32
## What Does it Mean to Be a Trailblazer?
*Rochelle Odesser*

According to the dictionary, a trailblazer is a pioneer who creates a path in uncharted territory. To be a trailblazer is to be a leader willing to encourage and help someone else on the journey. I had not considered myself a trailblazer or a leader, but over time, I realized that I have those qualities.

My journey began when I was looking for work that had meaning for me and permitted me to control my time and compensation, which allowed me to provide for my family and a nice lifestyle. I wanted to work where there were opportunities for me to learn and grow.

I had several jobs before becoming a financial advisor, and none felt right. I was a teacher and an administrative assistant in many different types of businesses. I learned more about myself and what was important to me from those positions. Even writing the words "became a financial advisor" sounds right because it is something that I have grown into over the 40 years that I have worked in this field.

When I began, it was a job. My work was to talk to people, find out about their financial situation, and enroll them in life insurance or some mutual funds. I was to review a person or family's financial situation and find holes that products could fill. I was never quite comfortable in that role. There was more that the industry could be doing to help people. However, at that time, the infrastructure of the financial services industry was not set up to help the middle class, only the wealthy.

It was after several different jobs in the business that I found my home and my mentor. I had more clarity in how I wanted to work and was in the right place to work the way I wanted. This opening allowed me to formulate my vision of being an advisor to people and set up a system that would accomplish that. I had to trust that I would develop the process and the right people to work with. I now collaborate with younger women in my firm and help them become their version of what they want.

Life is truly a journey; we must be flexible, adjust to new circumstances, and keep moving.

---

**Rochelle Odesser** is a Certified Financial Planner (CFP) and holds securities and insurance licenses in multiple states. Rochelle joined the team at Madison Planning Group in 2006. In her role as Vice President, she continues to help individuals and families plan for the future, manage debt, handle complex family situations, and more.

"I help people in transition, examining their next steps and want to ensure their financial situation will allow them to move ahead with purpose and prosperity."

LinkedIn: @rochelle-odesser

# TRAILBLAZER SECRET #33
## Inspired Healing: Revealing the Hidden Dangers of Health Foods, Redefining Wellness, and Advocating Patient Empowerment
### *Sally K. Norton*

How does a book about a little-known topic by an unknown author ignite a counter-cultural movement? In a matter of months, tens of thousands of readers have discovered that routine use of many of their beloved "health foods" may be causing their health problems. The problem with those foods is that they contain a natural toxin called oxalic acid, or oxalate. Plants make oxalates, and too much in our diets leads to trouble.

Despite my nutrition degree from Cornell and my public health master's, I learned this lesson the hard way. Over 40 years of dedication to healthy living created chronic problems with joint pain, fatigue, crippling foot problems, chronic gut issues, and a sleep disorder that ended my career.

In response to another odd, life-disrupting symptom, a Google search in 2009 led me to The Vulvar Pain Foundation, founded by a modern hero, Joanne Yount. Joanne teaches a low-oxalate diet for pelvic pain, which I tried out of desperation. However, it took me three more years to truly grasp the situation, alter my diet, and finally witness the transformative magic of reversing a broader set of health problems.

Upon my surprising recovery, I felt compelled to understand why. With newfound well-being, I explored the medical literature for an explanation, where little known oxalate intricacies across two centuries of research were hiding. What I found compelled inspired me to share through writing and speaking, culminating in a coaching practice.

My research, teaching, and consulting yielded pioneering insights. I coined the term "oxalate overload" to describe relentless high oxalate Intake and the health calamities that emerge from it. Oxalate overload is widespread. Yet a few simple dietary adjustments can make a significant difference. Even slightly reducing oxalate-rich foods can help. It's becoming clear that much of what we call' aging' may result from too many years of oxalate coming from trusted foods.

In my book Toxic Superfoods, I condensed years of work into a practical, accessible format. It simplifies a complex message for easy application. Anyone can try the affordable, non-invasive lifestyle changes I suggest. Adopters are achieving sought-after results after years of frustration.

The strong and positive reception for my work gives me great hope that I can make a lasting difference in improving human health.

---

**Sally K. Norton,** MPH, holds a nutrition degree from Cornell University and a master's in Public Health. Her book "Toxic Superfoods: How Oxalate Overload is Making You Sick-and How to Get Better" is available everywhere books are sold.

Instagram: @sknorton and @toxicsuperfoods_oxalate_book
YouTube: "Better with Sally K. Norton"
Website: sallyknorton.com

# TRAILBLAZER SECRET #34
## Trailblazing A New Path in Transforming Stress
### *Sara and Rachel Nakamura*

In a world paralyzed by uncertainty during the global shutdown, stress remains a constant companion. Overwhelm has reached a breaking point, impacting health, relationships, and work worldwide. As well-being consultants with a background in hands-on massage therapy, Rachel and I had to adapt to a "hands-off" approach to help our clients and those around us. This inside-out approach became apparent, especially after the suicide of our colleague. We recognized a common thread amongst thousands of clients: stress was deeply rooted in re-occurring dis-ease, affecting nearly all aspects of their lives, creating a stress cycle.

This realization inspired us to develop simple yet effective two-minute techniques to transform our client's five components of stress: Body, Emotions, Actions, Thoughts, and Triggers (B.E.A.T.T.). Breaking through their barriers by rewiring a new holistic path in transforming stress with a mind and body approach to tackle any challenge. This ICARE system forms the foundation of our bestselling book, **"Stressed Out and Don't Know What to Do?"**

Whatever problems arise, incorporate 5 Simple Steps.

**I.C.A.R.E.**
Go... **I**nside yourself - The solution is within you
**C**ontain - Cut the negativity
**A**wareness - What's really happening
**R**ealign - Prioritize your needs
**E**nergize- Make your decision with confidence

Even in the present day, the world remains in a state of flux, and stress is an ever-present challenge. The tragic loss of our dear friend Kat shook our community again; however, the tools of our ICARE system has allowed us to navigate these challenging times more effectively.

*Stop being stuck in stress; take the opportunity to...*
**Break the Stress Cycle Before Stress Breaks You!**

---

**Sara and Rachel Nakamura**, both best-selling authors, draw from their 30 years of combined experience in overcoming their own personal and professional challenges. As StressXperts, they are dedicated to helping heart-centered clients break through the stress cycle.

Email: info@stressxpert.com
Gift: FreeGiftFromSara.com
Instagram: @sara_stressxpert

# TRAILBLAZER SECRET #35
## A New Focus, A New Direction
### *Sereda Fowlkes*

Whether you're an entrepreneur, a homemaker, or a business owner, I firmly believe that you bear a responsibility and commitment to excel in whatever you pursue. Additionally, maintaining optimal health is essential for fulfilling your purpose during your time on this earth. Your unique skills constitute your mission, and your individuality renders you irreplaceable. I've realized that while money is undoubtedly necessary, the true wealth most people seek is good health.

Money can procure many things but cannot buy health or the inclination to prioritize self-care. Despite varying physical and mental circumstances, it's evident that a significant number of individuals neglect their well-being. Optimal health provides opportunities to dream, whether it's spontaneous travel or the ability to engage with children and grandchildren.

Taking a leap of faith, I ventured beyond my comfort zone to become a Certified Wholistic Health Coach. Working with those who've lost hope due to illness has been rewarding. My training emphasized identifying the root causes of sickness. In acknowledging that, I realized there are various reasons for health-related challenges. Decades of symptom masking have perpetuated the same problems society has settled for.

My mission is to deliver nutrition and improved health to those willing to embrace it. Once the eagerness to change is present, the subsequent steps are crucial. Consistent effort is necessary to achieve the desired health outcomes. I encourage you not to shortchange yourself—embrace good health and savour its benefits. Why Be Sick?

**Sereda Fowlkes** is a Speaker, Author and Wholistic Health Coach working with people to encourage lifestyle changes for better health. She addresses the effects of emotions, food choices, nutrition, and ways to take control of your health.

Sereda is a results-driven entrepreneur who loves to see things get done. Jim Rohn says, "Discipline is the bridge between goals and accomplishment." She wants you to be motivated to move from where you are to where you want to be in your health.

Email: sereda@seredafowlkes.com
LinkedIn: @SeredaFowlkes
Website: healthyjourneyforwellness.com

# TRAILBLAZER SECRET #36
## Lessons from a Burnt-Out Therapist
*Shannon Gander*

I muttered sheepishly into my cellphone, "Yvonne, I can't make lunch today." I never cancelled my plans. "I'm lying on my living room floor, crying, and can't get myself up." Unphased, she responded, "Good, it's about time! Stunned, I wondered what kind of friend says that. I later learned it's someone who cares deeply about your well-being and can see when you can't see yourself. She saw the burnout signs, but I did not. Therapist, heal thyself.

I grew up with self-employed parents. My Dad worked until he dropped dead (literally). Our dining room table was a sea of textbooks. Mom went to university the year I started grade one. She completed her PhD then opened a clinic. Later, we became business partners. Working lunches were standard practice. Mom is 78 years old and still practices.

After the day I couldn't get off the floor to meet my friend (who I later found out was dying of cancer), I vowed to find a different path. I had to mastermind a life where I could still work passionately caring for others without living on the edge of burnout and missing out on life.

My secrets? Paying attention to my signs, these are feeling rushed when I am not late, headaches and sugar cravings. I'm less present and irritable and fantasize about time for myself balanced with doses of guilt and shame for not doing enough. When friends start an invitation with, "I know you're super busy but…", I take this as a warning that I am giving off "busy energy" that disconnects me from others.

I've learned not to take these signs as flaws but as information. I've also developed a system of daily strategies for burnout prevention and letting go of balance to embrace work-life boundaries. Most valuable, I've had accountability partners to keep me on track.

If you are passionate about work, I encourage you to use curiosity without judgment; otherwise, you might miss critical signs. See these as information, consider reaching out, and please be kind to yourself as you find your way. I can tell you, you're worth it!

---

**Shannon Gander** is a global mental health speaker, trainer, and counsellor. She is the founder and Director of Life Work Wellness, a company that empowers individuals, workplaces, and communities to co-create cultures of mental well-being. Shannon is sought after for her expertise in mental wellness and resiliency and how, through storytelling and humour, she can inspire an audience to take small daily actions that have significant returns on their relationships, energy, and joy.

LinkedIn: @shannongander
Website: lifeworkwellness.ca

# TRAILBLAZER SECRET #37
## Key Principles for Success
### Shelly Lynn Hughes

As a seasoned entrepreneur with 25 years of experience, my enduring success is attributed to three key principles: collaboration, embracing failure and change, and fostering trust in teams and leadership.

Collaboration:
In today's interconnected business landscape, collaboration is paramount. Clear communication serves as the cornerstone for effective collaboration. Establishing transparent communication lines, whether internal or external, ensures everyone is well-informed. Clearly defined roles and regular updates foster synergy, minimize misunderstandings, and lead to better outcomes. Diversity within teams and partnerships is a strength, bringing varied perspectives and ideas, fostering creative problem-solving, and expanding opportunities.

Effective collaboration also improves problem-solving and decision-making. Multiple minds working together identify blind spots and biases, resulting in more informed decisions. Constructive feedback and diverse perspectives lead to thorough issue analysis and superior solutions.

Embracing Failure and Change:
Success requires an acceptance of failure as a natural part of the entrepreneurial journey. Failure is not a setback but a signal that the original plan needs adjustment. Flexibility and a willingness to change course are essential for finding optimal solutions.

Trusting your Team, Leadership, and Trusting Yourself:
Strong leadership is a requirement for a strong business. A

leader who can inspire and guide teams, set clear goals, and ensure accountability is essential. They should also be willing to delegate and empower team members while providing support and resources. Trust your gut and your decision-making. Listen to your team and their suggestions. Always hire people who are experts in their fields. You may disagree with them because your gut told you so, but hear them out... you hired them for a reason.

A trailblazing entrepreneur embraces collaboration, possesses effective communication skills, and builds diverse teams and partnerships. These qualities are essential for navigating the complexities of the modern business world. By adhering to these principles, entrepreneurs can foster enduring success and make a significant impact in the dynamic business landscape.

---

**Shelly Lynn Hughes** is a passionate multi-business owner and founder of both collaborative projects, Fresh Magazine and Pursuit 365, fusing inspirational stories and uplifting content from influential people wearing different hats worldwide.

Shelly believes that making a good imprint on the world and that collaboration, kindness and support are imperative to the well-being of our families, communities and businesses.

Facebook: @shellylynnhughes
Instagram: @pursuit_365
Website: pursuit365.com

# TRAILBLAZER SECRET #38
## Stop Sabotaging Your Greatest Potential
### *Susan Cumberland*

WARNING: Do not do these things if you want to be successful at Life and Business.

1. Don't neglect your physical and emotional health. Make this your top priority!
2. Don't let people walk all over you. Set boundaries!
3. Don't fly by the seat of your pants. Set measurable goals. Set an action plan and stick to it.
4. Don't deny a drug or alcohol addiction. Seek help and do what it takes to overcome this. It will destroy everything in your life.
5. Don't submit to self-destructive habits. Create positive habits and repeat them day after day.
6. Don't be a flake! If you make a promise, keep it. If you make a goal, achieve it.
7. Don't procrastinate and let things fester. These habits will kill your business, create anxiety, and destroy personal and professional relationships. Get difficult tasks/conversations done! Meet them head-on. Move on quickly.
8. Don't be too proud. If you make a mistake, own it, learn from it, and let others know you will do better next time. Accept feedback graciously.
9. Don't be an overachieving perfectionist. Accept that what you have done is enough.
10. Don't be a victim who blames others for your failure. Sure, you will have difficult circumstances that seem unfair. Take charge and control what you can. Recognize the things you cannot control and accept them.
11. Don't gossip about others behind their back. No one will trust you.

12. Don't hang out with deadbeats or toxic people. Learn to recognize who brings you down and who builds you up. Surround yourself with people who support you.

My favorite quote is by Michael Gerber, who wrote the E-Myth [Entrepreniual Myth]: "All you need to do is take your life seriously. To create it intentionally. To actively make your life into what you wish it to be."

---

**Susan Cumberland** says she is the perfect example of "nobody's perfect." She's made mistakes and has scars to prove it. 25 years of entrepreneurship. 23 years of motherhood. B.A. Secondary Ed, M.A Educational Leadership and Counselling. She's lived and learned and wants to share her life experience with young entrepreneurs

Linktree: linktr.ee/susancumberland
linktr.ee/schooliseasycalifornia
linktr.ee/schooliseasyvancouver

# TRAILBLAZER SECRET #39
## Goals are Key to Success
### *Susan Fox Dixon*

When I retired after 30 years as a trial attorney, I wanted to write but did not know where to start. So, I began by setting goals. I set my long-term goal to publish a specific book. Then, I set out short-term goals. When will I finish the book? What are my daily goals? How much will I write each working day? Those goals clarified my ideas, focused my efforts, and allowed me to use my time and resources better and more productively.

Top-level executives, athletes, and high achievers in all fields set goals. Goals gave me a long-term vision and short-term motivation. By setting clearly defined goals, I was better prepared to achieve them, giving me self-confidence and motivation to succeed.

Emmit Smith, former Hall of Fame NFL football player who became a motivational speaker, said, "It is only a dream until you write it down. Then it becomes a goal."

Once you set lifetime goals, develop a five-year plan of smaller goals toward your lifetime plan. Then, create a one-year plan, a six-month plan, and a one-month plan. Each phase will have smaller goals to work toward achieving your lifetime goals. Periodically review your short-term and long-term goals and modify them to reflect your changing priorities and experience.

"You are never too old to set another goal or dream a new dream." C.S. Lewis

**Susan Fox Dixon** was born and raised in Long Beach, California. She is an author of children's books and cookbooks, a blogger, a home chef, and an avid crafter. She currently lives in Huntington Beach, California. She is a wife, mom to four adult children and grandma to nine grandchildren.

Susan worked for 30 years as a trial attorney. After a demanding career, she retired early and began writing. She has written children's picture books and middle-grade and young-adult books. She has written craft books, cookbooks, advice books and guidebooks for kids moving out or going away to college with tips like credit cards are not free money, how to set goals, and how to get a job. She also has interesting blogs on various topics on her website. On this site, you can also sign up to receive the gift of a spicy food recipe and a chocolate dessert recipe.

Website: susanfoxdixon.com

# TRAILBLAZER SECRET #40
## I Found My Power
### *Susan Mielke*

I am sharing my story on how I overcame many years of being power-overed, gas-lit, and verbally/emotionally abused to successfully run a company traditionally dominated by men for men.

My 1st step was to take two courses, one on forgiveness, to forgive myself (to stop thinking things were my fault or trying to fix things only to find myself on a hamster wheel), and another to learn passive techniques to step away from the control and bullying. At the same time, I did not want to make my planned journey, to take over the company, obvious. I knew I was better equipped in every capacity but wasn't given the chance - if my opinion differed I was stupid and lived in a fantasy world.

Following are strategies I used:
(1) Silent patience while listening, absorbing, researching all that can be, and asking questions – it's incredible how much people will tell you when they like hearing their voice.
(2) Stop engaging in unhealthy communication – if a person is unwilling to listen to a different perspective or idea, don't waste time trying to convince or defend.
(3) Do not take others' behaviours personally – that's their issue, not yours.
(4) Avoid nonconstructive criticism and seek constructive criticism – if you don't know, how will you learn/grow/adjust? What we think we're conveying may be received otherwise via body language, tone, or our chosen words.
(5) Be comfortable walking away confidently without apology.
(6) Be assertive, not aggressive.

(7) Lead by example – if my kids aren't proud of what I'm doing, I don't do it.

(8) Never emotionally react -- walk away, think about both sides of the issue, and remove all emotion, adjectives, and adverbs before responding.

A key factor I discovered in finding my power was to facilitate – people absorb far more and are more creative when being part of the solution. I didn't have this opportunity until I broke free. From my experience, I knew to ask leading questions, not to "tell." There is greater ownership when individuals understand it's not all about them on the job but about them as part of a team to get the job done. Greater teamwork becomes a healthier and more desirable company, enabling the company greater freedom with its clients – everyone benefits.

---

Having spent many years travelling as an international athlete, **Susan Mielke** can now be found hanging with her fierce and delightful kids, attending concerts, games, and plays, or planning her next adventure abroad. Susan is a four-time Women of Distinction nominee, trainer and coach, and now principal/president in construction labour contracting.

Email: mielke.susan@gmail.com

# TRAILBLAZER SECRET #41
## The Infinite Journey
### *Tanya Steele*

*I stood, tied to a tree, my arms bound tightly behind me, the barrel of an automatic rifle aimed unwaveringly at my head. Three men, their faces hard and their voices loud and demeaning, insulting me "you're a stupid lady". They seem to grow more menacing as they questioned my purpose.*
*(Summer 2001 during Crisis Training)*

My life is one of privilege, for which I am deeply grateful. Having grown up in Canada with loving, supportive parents, accessible education, and freedom of choice. But soon, I would be a world away from this life, I would be facing a brutally different reality.

My medic background paved my way into a program for "Crisis Training" designed for NGO volunteers deployed into a war-torn region. I was young with a successful business, and even though this was a pivotal time in my career, I prepared my staff, so I could go on a mission, to bring relief, supplies, and a measure of hope to those in need. I began to prepare and packed for 16 days of training in Europe.

Upon arrival, the immersion into the training was immediate. The initial moments brought unexpected revelations. We were stripped of our modern luxuries. My safe haven of communication with family and friends was severed; my phone, laptop, and personal comforts no longer existed. They were about to plunge us into a world of scenarios designed to mirror the realities of a worn-torn country.

We were urged to embrace the process, to step willingly into the challenges of the people living with uncertainty and instability. With commitment, I embraced it all – from changing a flat tire on a desolate road to crossing foreign borders and sharing meals with locals.

As a young woman in a land where gender rights were scarce, I faced a sharp learning curve, enduring insults, being spit on and generally dismissed as a person. Stripped of the freedom I'd always known, I had to recalibrate my sense of self. Adapting meant ceding control, mastering the art of silence, observation, and subtly influencing my male team members.

The journey spiraled deeper each day. Nights punctuated by blaring speakers mimicking bombs, gunfire and our instructors screaming at us to run for safety. As I was trying to make sense of the chaos I was pulled from my bunk and landed hard on the floor. They urged us to flee to a WWII-era bunker for safety. Confused and bruised my team huddled, waiting for a sign that we could move back to our bunks. Returning to our beds brought relief and apprehension. After what seemed like minutes, we were awakened again with an order to leave immediately.

Exhausted both mentally and physically, we began hiking to our destination, a refugee camp, carrying a backpack of medical supplies for them. Through it all, my spirit remained unyielding, until a beautiful walk in the forest unraveled into a sinister trap by our trainers. Suddenly a group men came out of the bush, each man armed with a rifle, pointing at us. They demanded we get down on our knees, which we did without resistance. We had nothing left to offer; we had already run out of money to give in such a scenario. Yet these men seemed interested in being compensated. The men looked at each of us, carefully calculating what they wanted. Being the only woman, two of the men grabbed my arms and began to drag me into the bush. My friends called out my name, begging for my release which the gunman refused. They lifted me from the ground and pushed my back against a tree, tying my arms behind me. I pleaded for my life. They raised their weapons and put them against my head. Doubts began to surface in mind; was this still a training simulation. I questioned my motivation for why I was there - I had worked for months to pay for this trip, I had been spat on, kicked, disrespected, left hungry, tired, and bruised. I wanted to make a difference in people's lives, Was all of this worth it? Deep consideration and this internal dialogue left me grappling with the validity of my purpose.

Tearful and trembling, I felt an unfathomable peace come over me, then I heard a still small voice in my heart. It reminded me that even these people are afraid, struggling, and in need of help. My focus shifted from the end game, our destination into the refugee camp, to being present in this moment on my journey. I began to ask myself, what help, medical supplies or kindness could we offer these men and their families.

Today, my journey has culminated the birth of "What If One Educates," a testament to the belief that a single person, in a single moment, can make a difference with one choice. As the echoes of that fateful day reverberate in my memory, I'm reminded that the path to success is not measured by grand achievements, but paved with courage, compassion, and the unwavering belief that even in the face of uncertainty, a simple act of kindness can transform lives. As my company's name suggests, I want you to consider the ripple effect of a single choice, a single gesture in your journey.

**Tanya Steele** is a former EMR and is now a trainer, safety advisor and Podcast Host of Safety Debris. Utilizing her experience in business, construction, mining, tourism, municipal and the film industry, she helps owners, supervisors, OHS committee members and HR leaders understand and implement safety in the workplace. Tanya is an expert in Joint Health & Safety Committee training, educating and rejuvenating company meetings to make them more effective & collaborative.

In 2018 she started "What If One Educates" to train other leaders on how to train their workers more effectively, with the concept that one person can make a difference in one person's life and possibly save that life. Her goal is to help raise the next generation of trainers that are fun, engaging and impactful!

LinkedIn: @tanyarsteele
Podcast: safetydebris.podbean.com
Website: johsc.ca and tanyasteele.ca

# TRAILBLAZER SECRET #42
## We Can Do It All, But Do We Want to Be?
### *Tina Collura*

As an entrepreneur, you start a business because you are passionate about your products or services and know you can help others succeed by adding value to their lives.

In the beginning (and perhaps even now), you had to wear multiple hats: The Marketing Manager, The Salesperson, and The Lead Generator. You may also be the Production Manager and many others. In short, you were the business.

Initially, you are pumped full of adrenaline because your business is booming, and you are on cloud nine because your vision is becoming a reality. You also slowly realize you are exhausted and missing precious time with friends and family. You are working hard to build your business and feel you cannot divide your attention and still succeed.

In my first four months of business, I had to ask myself: what is working, what isn't, and what can I do better? It became undeniable that the things that were not working were those I did not love to do. I had to ask myself If I was ready to give up that work (Control) and delegate it to someone who did love to do those things. As a business owner, we can be our greatest assets and our greatest enemy. We can all admit that giving up control is one of the hardest things to do.

As a person who has led teams and spoken to many organizations about the importance of having the right people, processes, and technology in place, I advise my clients to start with these three steps to help them manage the deluge of work piling up:

Step 1 – DELEGATE – find someone who can take on some of your administrative work to start.

Step 2 – PRIORITIZE – Identify what needs to happen now and in the next 30-60-90 days.

Step 3 – SET UP THE RIGHT BOUNDARIES – If people are coming to you with problems, instead of saying: "I'll take care of that," advise them to send you an email with the details and encourage them to come up with some solutions. By encouraging your people to take this initiative, you will see them take greater pride in their work and will help them build their confidence.

By doing these three steps, you will reduce your need to control everything, and it will help you manage your time and efficiency so that you can focus on the things you are passionate about and where your expertise shines.

*"Sometimes, the most powerful act of leadership a business owner makes Is the release control, trust in the talent and capabilities of their team and steer the ship towards success."*
   T. Collura.

---

**Tina Collura** is an Award-Winning Productivity Coach, Business Growth Consultant and Motivational Speaker. Tina shows business owners how to develop & implement business growth strategies that will help them increase their revenue streams and attract new clients.

## Client Testimonials

"Tina is a firecracker that helped me get Lazar focused with the core messages in my branding, on my website and in my new videos."

~ D. Stewart

"The 8-week SYBG program has been beneficial to ease my anxiety and doubt about starting my own business"

~ T. Rennie

"Tina helped me grow from a solopreneur to the hiring of 2 new employees with Tina's HR Operational Experience in 4 months!

~M. Tucker

"Tina helped me grow my income from 3 figures to 6 figures in less than six months"

~A. Sweeney

"Not only did she motivate my team and me personally, she helped my team exceed our sales goals within 6 months after one session! Since we had that session, five of our team members earned promotions in our business! Absolutely incredible!"

~S. Acquisto

Email: tina@seeyourselfgrow.com
LinkedIn: @seeyourselfgrowwithtina
Website: seeyourselfgrow.com

# The Following Pages Contain
# ***BONUS MATERIAL***

# *Diane Rolston Interviewed by Jack Canfield*

JACK CANFIELD: Hi, I'm Jack Canfield. You may know me as the co-author of the 'Chicken Soup for the Soul' series, the book 'The Success Principles,' and featured teacher in the movie 'The Secret.' I'm here with Diane Rolston, and we'll have a great conversation about her amazing work in the world. Welcome, Diane.

DIANE ROLSTON: Thank you. A pleasure to be here with you.

JACK CANFIELD: I'm glad you're here. Tell us a little bit about what you do.

DIANE ROLSTON: Well, Jack, I do two things. First, I've had great success as a certified life and business coach. I specialize in coaching high-level dynamic women as well as entrepreneurs. I find that they prioritize success over their satisfaction in life, so I help them rebalance their life while still getting to their goals quickly and powerfully.

Because of my work, I'm often brought in with my expertise to do keynotes, so fee-paid keynotes. I talk to women's groups. I speak to conferences, associations, corporations, and such. They have me basically come in to be the person to inspire them, to get the event going, and to share some of my strategies on leadership, success, business and life.

Because of that piece, the coaching and the speaking and how I run my business, I've had people come to me and say, "Diane, how do you do all that you do and still have a life and have a family?" I'm married with two kids.

As you probably know, many different things connect to someone's success. But one of the main things is that I have really, really great virtual assistants that helped me behind the scenes.

When people like these high-achieving women, business owners say, "Diane, how can I do that, too? How do you hire them? How do you train them? What do you delegate?" Then, I tell them, "Oh, well, I actually do more than just admin tasks." Because a lot of people think, "Oh, a virtual assistant does your email and calendar."

Instead, I do other things, higher-level tasks and projects with them things like they're going to support my:
- Social media content creation
- Management
- Technology
- Creating graphics
- Audio and video editing

All these different things a busy business owner must do every day and doesn't have time to do.

That's how the second business was formed. I now consult, coach, and provide virtual assistant services for the busy business owners I work with.

JACK CANFIELD: You have virtual assistants you've trained and help people hire? Is that what you're saying?

DIANE ROLSTON: Yeah, I share many of my systems, my processes, and how I've been doing my coaching and speaking business with my clients. Plus, I'm a podcaster. I have books, run summits, and a women's community called Dynamic Women.

With all that, they say, "Okay, cool, we can just take that." It becomes straightforward for them. It's like an easy recipe to follow. It's like, A-B-C 1-2-3. I connect all the dots for them.

JACK CANFIELD: It's interesting because I do a lot of consulting with entrepreneurs, usually people who are just starting small businesses, solo entrepreneurs, solopreneurs, whatever. They always say, "Well, what's the next thing I should do?" I say, "Hire an assistant." The best thing you can do about anything is hire an assistant. It can be a virtual assistant or someone local, whichever. But half of my staff started as interns for free as assistants in my company, got to know them, worked well, kept them around to now they move on up, whatever. But it's so important.

Do you find that many people feel like they don't deserve an assistant? They don't feel worthy of it? Or do they feel like they can't afford it?

DIANE ROLSTON: All those things. All those pieces. I think it's based on what society has drilled into them. This picture of this hard-working 80-hour-a-week solopreneur that means:
- "You can't afford to have it yet."
- "You're not allowed to have it yet."
- "You shouldn't do it. Just work hard."

But that's not why people get into doing their own business. We're not meant to do every aspect on that organizational chart. We are meant to stay in our core competencies.

JACK CANFIELD: You're passionate about what you do. Why so passionate? Where'd that come from?

DIANE ROLSTON: Great question. I want people to awaken. I want to provoke them to what's possible. I want to unleash the dynamic version of themselves. When I'm brought in to do a keynote, whether it's an opening or closing, whatever it may be, I often share one of the struggles that I had and one of the biggest learnings, which is to stop measuring your life according to your success.

What happens is people do that, and then they get into this place of, "I'm only happy when I have success." But once they reach the success, they realize, "Wow, success is fleeting." Then they chase that next goal, that next high of achievement, but then they realize, "I'm not even satisfied inside." That's sad.

I see it a lot in high-level, dynamic women and entrepreneurs who end up being overworked, overwhelmed, and pulled in a million directions. It's like they're on that hamster wheel, right? It's just going faster and faster and faster and faster. Eventually, they fall off. Instead, I encourage them, "Measure your life according to your satisfaction."

If I were coaching you, Jack, I'd say, "Hey, let's use this tool. Let's look at all the areas of life, and what do you want in every area?" That's one of the most challenging questions people have to answer. You probably know it in your world. Most people ask, "What do you mean 'What do I want?'"

To see the visual when they can score their satisfaction and ask, "In the future, what do you want in these areas?" and when they get really crystal clear on that, they go, "Oh, this is great. I can choose what I want for myself," not just what society has dictated is successful, what society has decided that just confines and defines us. I want to be able to bring that to more people. That's why donating my books and proceeds to women in shelters is important to me.

JACK CANFIELD: Oh, good for you. There are a lot of people out there who say they coach people, they help them live more successful lives, whatever. I think you've answered part of this by talking about satisfaction. But what makes your work different or unique compared to all the other people who are out there doing that?

DIANE ROLSTON: Yeah, you're very right, Jack. When I work with people, I give them strategies. I give them ideas. I give them a clear plan. I pull out of them what they want. But a lot of other coaches say they do that, too.

I think the difference is I'm still in the game. I'm not on the sidelines. I'm doing the coaching. I'm working on myself. I am constantly like, "Okay, how can I be more satisfied," and I'm doing all the things in my business and at least overseeing them.

I'm still in the game where I find many other people who don't have the experience I do, or they were doing this 10 years ago or even just a few years ago. But if you're on the sidelines, you don't know what has changed in your ideal clients' lives their businesses, with technology.

Because I'm still in it, I understand. I can relate to my clients, to the struggles they've had, to the fears they have. Because of that, I also feel it's really important that my clients get me when they hire me. They get me. They get my consulting, my coaching, my speaking. They're not going to get someone under me.

That's probably part of why I have over 1000 five-star reviews on social media and other platforms. That's part of it.

I think the other piece I aim for is a complete transformation. Not, "Let's have a quick fix. Let's make this happen overnight." No. I want a full transformation, an entire shift so that it cannot just be in that specific situation but ripple out into other areas of life. Plus, they're a catalyst for change for others.

JACK CANFIELD: Now, you alluded to one of these things earlier, but I'll ask you again: you see a lot of challenges out there in the world that people are having. What do you see as the most common challenges? How do you help people address those and overcome them?

DIANE ROLSTON: Great question. It's funny because I love challenges. I grew up playing competitive sports. I have to create challenges for myself so I'm not bored. But I know you're speaking more about problems in this case, right? Obstacles that people face.

When I'm coaching one-on-one, in a group program, or even in a virtual session, I often hear from these high-level women and entrepreneurs that their challenges come up.

I'm going to share three challenges with you. I'm going to share some that are pretty much universal to all.

The first one is that you have to balance work and life. You probably already know it isn't true, and you're like, "That's a lie." These challenges are all lies. I'll tell the lie, and then I'll tell the truth. If you're looking at work and life, they won't be balanced. The reason being is work is only one of the areas of life. We need all areas of life, so people are always like, "Well, I'm never going to be able to balance that." For me, that was an eye-opener. I'm a little bit of an A-type, recovering perfectionist. When I saw that, I went, "Ah, no wonder life's not balanced." It's not going to be. Once I started looking at my whole life, all ten areas, that helped me to allot where my time is. For my clients, I'm like, "Okay, so now what do you want in all these areas? How do you want things to be when you have that clarity? Then you'll be able to put in the right amount of time, energy, and money." That's the first lie.

You spoke about the second lie earlier: you don't make enough, or you're not big enough to hire or delegate. That is such a lie. Now, maybe you know, your day one in your business, okay, like, "Let's figure out what you're going to do first." But entrepreneurs still believe they can't hire someone, as you've said. But the thing is that people are thinking, "Oh, they're too expensive." But what I found in my experience is that they're a lot less than you think they are, at least in my team. They're also very highly competent. When they're able to take things off your shoulders, you're going to have more time, more energy, and more money. You're going to be able to increase your revenue. The coolest thing is, what if the person you hired could earn you enough money to pay for themselves? That's the clincher there. That's what we're looking for.

The third challenge is something that I often see. It's usually in response to someone being offered a great opportunity. They'll say, I'm too busy to take on anything else. Now, they're too busy to take on the wrong things. They're too busy to take on the wrong things. They have time for the right things. But until they get clarity on the things they want in life, they will always say "Yes" to the wrong things and "No" to the right things. I've seen that happen with people getting kind of their dream opportunities. They have to say no because they don't have the time, the energy, or the money. That's just heartbreaking. So heartbreaking. In those moments, I want to say, "Come on, you got to do this." That is one of the final challenges that I see for people. They need clarity.

JACK CANFIELD: Cool. If I was sitting here watching this, and I was what I like to call a "right fit client," someone who could benefit from what you do, I would want to work with you. It's clear because you have the knowledge, skills, insights, and experience to help people at a deep level.

Do you have any parting thoughts about someone who's watching this that might encourage them or give them ideas about how they might work with you? Or why should they?

DIANE ROLSTON: I hope everyone watching will grab a pen, write this down, and take it in. Because this is one of the key things that I had to learn myself, and then it's kind of a way of shifting in the people I work with. That is, you can't do it all yourself. You can't do it all yourself. Right?

Jack, I want to ask you, you've never seen geese fly alone? No, right? They don't fly alone. They fly in a V. Now, why is that? Because they're in a flock or even a few, they're always in a V because they can fly further, faster, together.

You probably know in your industry and all the great work you've done, there's such benefit to having a leader who will draft the path for you. Also, to have those around you to be able to encourage you. But what I see oftentimes, sadly, in high-level women, in entrepreneurs is that they come in that place of like, "I'm going to do it," and they get burnt out.

They can't do it all. They may give up on their dream, which is sad. I'm hoping that those at home, those who are watching, think about, "Wow, okay, so what do I need? I need my flock. Where am I going to find some people around me?"

That's why I created the Dynamic Women Global Club. That's why I did group coaching masterminds because of the benefit of others around you so that when you reach adversity, you can come in with the group and have them support you.

You also need a good leader. Someone who can coach you through can guide you to make it much easier. I'm hoping that people stop being that lone wolf, the silo and that they embrace that more of a team mentality.

JACK CANFIELD: I saw something the other day. It said, "No one ever climbed Mount Everest without a team." You can't do it alone if you really want to get to the top. It's impossible. It will never happen.

First of all, thank you. You're very cool. Appreciate it.

DIANE ROLSTON: Thank you very much. You are, too.

JACK CANFIELD: No, it's good. I mean, you're all watching this; I will encourage you to get in touch with Diane. I think all the things you talked about, the challenges that people have, you can't do it, can't afford it, all that if you're living in that, and you probably are, you need to stop and work with her.

She can help take you from where you are to where you want to be. I love that you talk about all the different areas of our life because people say, "Balance work and home." Well, work at home, there's spiritual growth, family time, hobbies, taking care of yourself, and self-nurturing. Exercise. All those things have to come into play and having a life that can be fulfilling in all those areas of your life, which life is meant to be.

Diane is someone that can help you do that. I want to encourage you to take advantage of the fact that she's available in the world, can help you, and be part of that community she talks about that can give you the support you need to fly like the geese. I love it. Alright, thanks for tuning in, everybody.

*"Diane is an amazing woman that does incredible work helping women develop, especially entrepreneurs, high-level, high-performing women, develop holistic lives of balance. Not just balanced, but really balancing all the different aspects of your life, not just one thing, but so many parts of yourself, and working with assistance, and really helping you realize you can afford it, you cannot not afford it. I want to encourage you to reach out not only for her work, but also for the community that she's created for people who are part of that work going forward so you have a supportive community to take you to the next level. So anyway, take advantage for work, check out her website, check out her get in touch with her and I promise you, you'll be glad you did."*
~ **Jack Canfield**, Author and Motivational Speaker
Co-Creator of the "Chicken Soup for the Soul" book series
Featured teacher in the movie "The Secret"

## *What Stops Women from Blazing a Trail*

Have you ever felt like you had to fly under the radar, dumb yourself down, be less than yourself to make others comfortable, or not get a negative response?

Strong, assertive, confident, and successful women often have to or choose to fly under the radar or hide who they are, and it's ticking me off.

If you can relate, I am just like you. This topic comes from my personal experience as a woman who, at times, had to hide my true self, not speak up and choose to fly under the radar to fit in.

I've also seen this with my coaching clients, who definitely would raise their hand and say,

*"Yeah, I didn't share my ideas because they're never respected."*
*"People feel threatened by my questions."* or
*"I don't always try to win things because of how people will treat me after I succeed."*

**These phrases are what flying under the radar means.**

The idea of flying under the radar is not to be so high, strong, confident, successful, or win things so you don't get on other people's radar as someone to attack, cut down, gossip about, or dislike.

**I flew under the radar many times…**

This has been true for me most of my life.

It was true for me in sports when I was invited onto a boy's rep team for soccer. I was not accepted, and no one would partner with me. In my coed soccer league, I had very harsh insults, swear words and derogatory comments thrown at me when I would take the ball away from them. I was just 12 or 13. As my daughter is 12, I can't even believe the things that were said to me that are probably still being said to girls today.

In high school, when I ran for Student Council President, the other candidate tried to win by spreading vicious lies, attacking my character and making up sexual rumours. I still won, but at what cost? I had to repair my name and prove myself, and he continued to run his mouth about me even when I was doing a great job. When it came time to pick the class Valedictorian, I chose not to put my name forward (even though it was a dream of mine) because I feared I'd face the same from him, so instead, I decided to fly under the radar.

In many areas of my life, I was cut down or felt negativity from others because I'd been successful or confident. This is not me bragging. This is me speaking my truth in relation to you and hundreds of women I have coached on this topic.

If you are a woman who has felt this, then I get it. Sometimes it's just so tiring. It's so frustrating because we're just doing our best. We're doing what brings us joy, and we're using the gifts that God has given us, and then people want to be hurtful because they are jealous of us or threatened by us.

In corporate environments, I see women not putting their hands up for roles because if they do, they're potentially going to lose all of their friends they're currently working with. They don't go for positions. They don't ask for a raise because of what people will say about them.

Will they be treated differently? The answer usually is, "They will". **But we can't let that stop us!!!**

A few years back, maybe four or five years ago, I wanted to interview a bunch of women. Two of the requirements for the interviewees were making multiple six or seven-figures and being in a leadership role. In these interviews, I found that this diminishing of oneself concept kept coming up repeatedly: *Life is easier if I fly under the radar.* This made me so sad and pretty pissed off!

*This concept that life is easier and more enjoyable if I don't stick my neck out or if I don't win things* saddens me, and it also scares me. It saddens me because these women are not living at their full potential for fear of what other people will say, will do, or the repercussions.

There should not be repercussions to doing well. Yes, you win a sport, you win a game, you are the gold medallist, whatever it may be, there will be people who are jealous of you, and there will be people who wish they were you. However, in a workplace with coworkers, to have other people treat you differently or have it out for you or, in my case, other people in the industry coming after you. What kind of world are we in where we can't all do well ourselves? What if everyone just did well and stopped putting their negativity on others?

### Sad and scary

It saddens me because people, specifically women, are settling and playing small, me included because it was just easier. It's just easier not to be the one in the public eye.

Over the last few years, I have often felt like I have been pulled back. It takes a lot of stamina to stay visible; I don't know how some famous people do it. It takes a lot of emotional and mental stamina to be in the public eye, take criticism, and have people cutting you down for no reason. They don't even know you.

It saddens me that women don't feel like they can step up into these more significant roles and play big. It also saddens me for the women that are around them, who are watching them and thinking, *"Well, if she is not going for that, and she's more confident than me, more successful than me, or more experienced than me, then I shouldn't either."*

A trickling down negative effect. Plus, not just women to women or peer to peer, but what about the girls coming behind us, the future women who have fewer role models to look up to?

I know for me, in the teaching and coaching sides of things, many women do not hide themselves. In my network, looking for role models in that way is straightforward. There are a lot of great female speakers, but not enough diversity so that we all can see them. Not enough women are on the main stages.

When they get on the main stage, how often is she criticized? People complain about her outfit and voice and often say she's too confident.

That's the sad side.

Do you know what the scary side is? The frightening side is the lack of gender equality and pay equity; these things are not going to get any better if we continue to diminish ourselves. I know we're not doing this intentionally but out of survival. There's just so much going on. While it's different for everybody, an underlying factor is that women must continuously try to be perfect:

- *Moms*
- *Business owners*
- *Corporate Professionals*
- *Wives*
- *Friends*
- *Daughters*
- *Sisters*
- *Board members*

- *Volunteers*
- *Neighbours*
- *Insert your multiple labels here*

We're trying to be the perfect everything. It's not just that we're always trying, but it's expected. If we're making an effort to do all these things, how will we also show up to our fullest in these places when we know that there's a chance that people will take us down?

I once said to my business advisor, "I thought when I was more successful, brought in more money and had more clients, things would be easier." But the truth is, "New level, new devil". You don't even realize who will come out of the woodwork after you. I don't say this to scare you, but to create awareness of the reality of it.

**Don't fly under the radar!**

I don't want us to fly under the radar anymore. What I'd love to do is see us soar. BUT HOW?

What I have determined is we need to come together.

Are these true about you?
- You desire spending time with women ahead of you, so you grow and learn how to collapse time
- You want to be inspired by others, so you can be stretched to achieve more at a higher level
- As a strong woman, you also require a soft space to land, so you can feel heard and supported
- You need a solid group of peers, so you don't have to lead all the time and instead can focus on yourself
- You value collaboration and everyone being able to have their own unique success without competition

Then read on…

I'm creating something special for high-level women. In preparation, I'm interviewing women who feel they have flown under the radar or that they have are making six or seven figures (I only say that because you've probably been established in your business or your company and have a lot of experience with this, and you're playing at that higher level).

If you want to be interviewed, email me directly at diane@dianerolston.com. Ideally, you've been in your position, company, or business for at least a few years, not just in the start-up stage, unless you've just come from having a business or career for more years. If you're in a leadership position or own your own time, and you've had an experience where you felt, "It would be easier just to lie low a little bit, not to put myself out there." I'd like to talk to you, too.

I'll share the research results with those who are part of the interview. I will also bring all these ladies together for a connection call and group discussion where I will share some solutions.

In wrapping this section up, even though it may sometimes feel safer to fly under the radar, connect back with your passion, your values, and your purpose. It's worth it in the end for your own satisfaction and the massive impact you will make when you SOAR HIGH!

# "YOU'RE DYNAMIC! BE UNAPOLOGETICALLY YOU!"

~ Diane Rolston

## *One Final Message*

Congratulations!

You did it! You now know more than 42 stories and secrets to be a trailblazer. You should be proud of yourself! You have invested in yourself with your personal development, and you will also grow professionally.

My mission with this book is threefold:
1. 1st to bring you a story a week from women you can relate to, be inspired by and connect with.
2. 2nd to give you actions you can implement to be even more of a trailblazer.
3. 3rd to bring to life the dream of many women to write a book.

I trust this book will motivate, inspire and empower thousands of women and then ripple out to those around you to impact tens of thousands with the trailblazer secrets.

My wish for you is that you…

## "DON'T FLY UNDER THE RADAR. CHOOSE TO BLAZE A TRAIL!"

By following the simple trailblazer secrets in this book, you can start to feel the reality of the life you have dreamt of.

**Just take one step, each day to be a trailblazer.
You got this Dynamic Woman!**
Mwah!
Diane

# YOU ARE A DYNAMIC WOMAN AND A TOP ACHIEVER!

# SPECIAL FREE BONUS GIFTS FOR YOU!

To help you achieve more success, there are free bonus resources for you at:

FreeGiftFromDiane.com

# Now it's your turn to Be a Trailblazer!

Manufactured by Amazon.ca
Bolton, ON